120 Ways to Annoy Your Mother
(And Influence People)

120 Ways to Annoy Your Mother (And Influence People)

by Ana Benaroya

 Thames & Hudson

Cover illustration and design by Ana Benaroya

First published in the United Kingdom in 2014 by Thames & Hudson Ltd,
181A High Holborn, London WC1V 7QX

British Library Cataloguing-in-Publication Data
A catalogue record for this book is available from the British Library

ISBN 978-0-500-29146-7

Printed and bound in China by Everbest Printing Co. Ltd

To find out about all our publications, please visit www.thamesandhudson.com.
There you can subscribe to our e-newsletter, browse or download our current catalogue,
and buy any titles that are in print.

TABLE OF CONTENTS

41. How to Be Fake
42. How to Read Someone's Mind
43. How to Spread World Peace
44. How to Speak Only in Metaphors
45. How to Pretend You are a Foreigner
46. How to Coexist with Bears
47. How to Be Interesting
48. How to Become an International Spy
49. How to Become Green with Jealousy
50. How to Control the Weather
51. How to Be a Wallflower
52. How to Save Money
53. How to Be a Health Nut
54. How to Become a Bodybuilder
55. How to Collect Cats
56. How to Ride a Horse
57. How to Turn Your Life into a Soap Opera
58. How to Be Clairvoyant
59. How Not to Lose Your Mind in a Crowded Subway Car
60. How to Be Really Awkward
61. How to Smile
62. How to Cook Eggs
63. How to Find a Way into Everyone's Heart
64. How to Be a Drama Queen
65. How to Have the Most Perfect Handwriting
66. How to Love Your Feet
67. How to Climb Really High
68. How to Be Magnanimous
69. How Literally to Become a Figure of Speech
70. How to Be the Worst Public Speaker
71. How to Understand Poetry
72. How to Start Your Own Fan Club
73. How to Moisturize
74. How to Bite Your Tongue
75. How to Be Thoughtful
76. How to Avoid Doing Laundry
77. How to Go on a Date
78. How to Create a Masterpiece
79. How to Melt Someone's Heart
80. How to Fly

(81) How to Get Taller
(82) How to Play the Piano
(83) How to Appreciate What You Have
(84) How to Be a Political Person
(85) How to Keep Up with the News and Not Get Depressed
(86) How to Live a Bohemian Lifestyle
(87) How to Deal with Money
(88) How to Become Really Flexible
(89) How to Tie the Most Perfect Ponytail
(90) How to Be a Picky Eater
(91) How to Enjoy Running
(92) How to Write a Love Letter
(93) How to Develop Inner Strength
(94) How to Understand Math
(95) How to Be Rebellious within the Confines of Society
(96) How to Become Rich
(97) How to Be Patient
(98) How to Balance Responsibility with Fun
(99) How to Become the Outdoorsy Type
(100) How to Be a Neat Freak
(101) How to Be Mentally Unbalanced
(102) How to Fight the Urge
(103) How to Talk About Your Feelings
(104) How to Be Mysterious
(105) How Always to Have Perfect Posture
(106) How to Fall From Grace
(107) How Always to Have the Answer
(108) How to Live in the Moment
(109) How to Know You're on the Right Path
(110) How to Remember Everything
(111) How to Write an Autobiography
(112) How to Be a Little Bad (Only a Little)
(113) How to Fall in Love
(114) How to Deal with Mean People
(115) How to Transition into Adulthood
(116) How to Deal with Change
(117) How to Resolve Inner Turmoil
(118) How to Become a Shadow of the Person You Used to Be
(114) How to Become a Morning Person
(120) How to Teleport

DRAW YOUR OWN FIREBALLS!!!

PRACTICE CHART (Keep track of your progress)

S	M	T	W	TH	F	S

DOES BREATHING FIRE BUILD YOUR SELF-ESTEEM?

WHO DO YOU *WANT* TO BREATHE FIREBALLS ON?

Person #1 _____   Person #2 _____   Person #3 _____

2
HOW TO MAKE YOUR HAIR LOOK HORRIBLE EVERY MORNING.
① Fight the urge to brush.
② Become a sweat and oil-producing MACHINE.
③ Use your hair as a high-security storage system. (Ex: Gum, leftover pizza, small creatures...)
④ Every three months cut off a chunk here and there. Aim for asymmetry.
(AT LEAST NINE MONTHS FOR BEST RESULTS)

DRAW YOUR WORST HAIR DAYS.

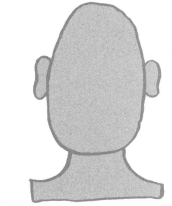

DATE:
FEELINGS:

DATE:
FEELINGS:

DATE:
FEELINGS:

DATE:
FEELINGS:

DATE:
FEELINGS:

DATE:
FEELINGS:

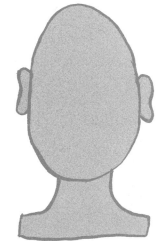

DATE:
FEELINGS:

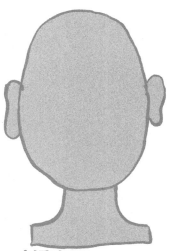

DATE:
FEELINGS:

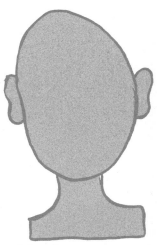

DATE:
FEELINGS:

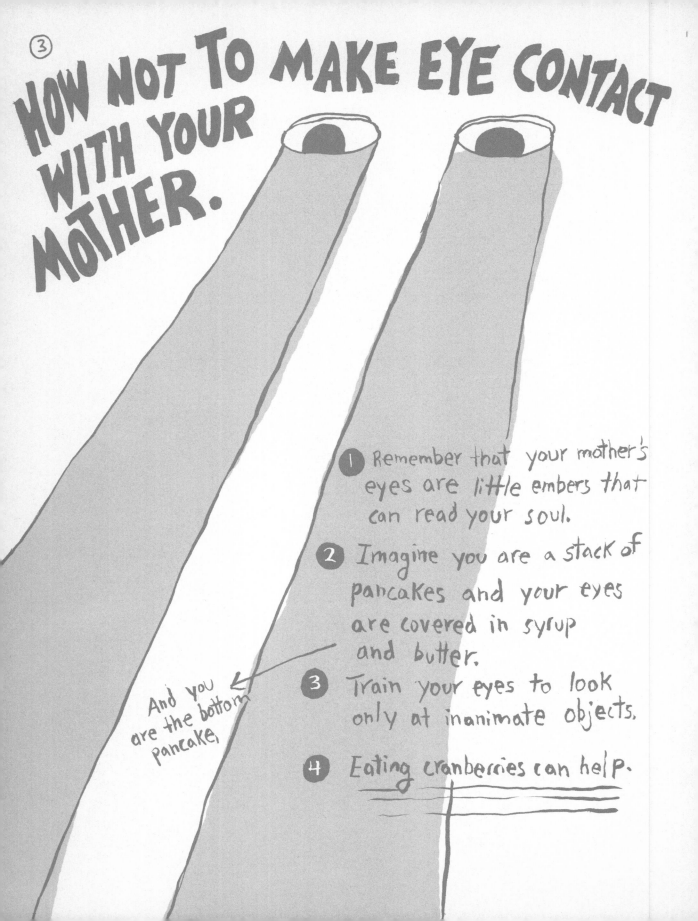

4
HOW TO WEAR TOO MUCH MAKEUP.
(AND BY TOO MUCH, WE MEAN JUST RIGHT!)
painted brows
dramatic eyes
high cheekbones
juicy lips
nice shoulders
1 Try to finish one stick of lipstick every day.
2 Makeup is food for your skin, don't let it starve! Apply at least three layers.
3 Consider using every color of the rainbow.
4 Think chunky peanut butter.

USE YOUR FINGERS TO PRACTICE WALKING UP AND DOWN THE STAIRS.

LIST YOUR FAVORITE THINGS TO DAYDREAM ABOUT WHILE WALKING DOWN STAIRS:

1
2
3
4

Draw something in this secret stair compartment.

WHAT DO STAIRS REMIND YOU OF?

EXERCISE FACT:
Stairs help build muscle and reduce social anxiety.

STAIRS FACT:
Stairs were invented in the year 43 by a woman named Olga.

HOW TO CHECK YOUR EMAIL 100x A DAY.

MAIL
INBOX
TRASH
SPAM

① Start checking while still in bed, right after your alarm goes off.

② Put your social life on perpetual hold. Email is now your one and only.

③ Never make eye contact with anyone. Keep your focus glued to an electronic device at all times.

④ Learn to connect spiritually with Wifi.

To:

From:

Subject:

PREDICT YOUR NEXT TWO EMAILS!!!

To:

From:

Subject:

⑦ HOW TO GROW A BEAUTIFUL GARDEN IN YOUR BATHTUB.

1. Bathtubs are surprisingly receptive to growing fauna and flora.

2. Select flowers and plants that will thrive in the particular climate of your bathroom.

3. Spend thirty minutes each day on garden upkeep. Give those flowers the tender loving care they deserve.

4. Should guests (or you) require to use the shower, point them in the direction of the garden hose.

DRAW YOUR DREAM GARDEN IN THIS DREAM BATHTUB.

HOW TO CURL YOUR EYE LASHES.

1 Condition them first with a potion of baby's tears and warm butter.

2 Massage them gently upwards for six to eight hours. Do not break.

3 Deep within your soul, imagine gravity has reversed and what was once down is now up.

4 Come up with a name for each eyelash, then mourn its death when it falls off.

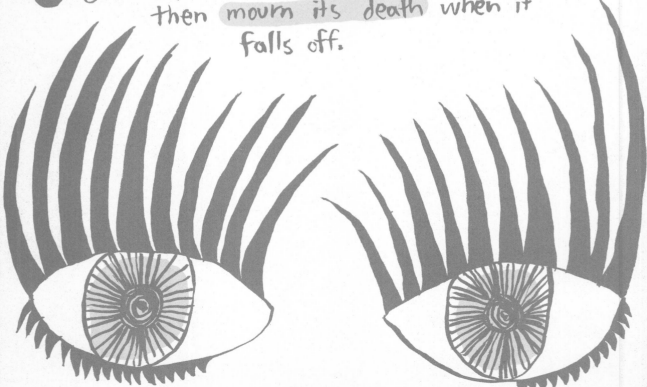

EYELASH CURL HEIGHT PROGRESS CHART

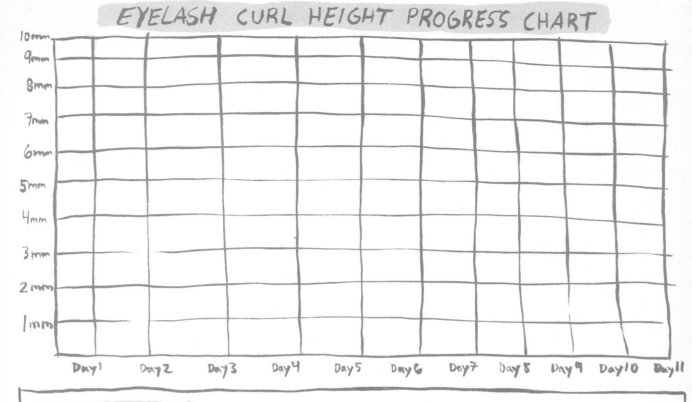

10mm
9mm
8mm
7mm
6mm
5mm
4mm
3mm
2mm
1mm

Day 1 Day 2 Day 3 Day 4 Day 5 Day 6 Day 7 Day 8 Day 9 Day 10 Day 11

EYELASH DIARY:

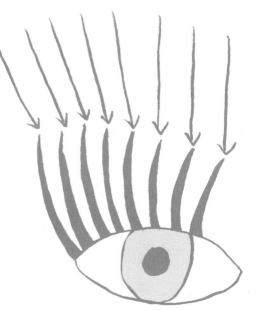

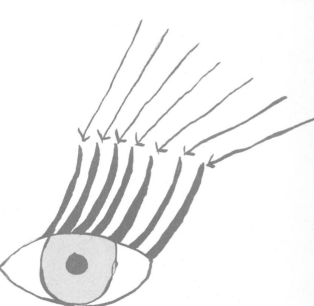

WRITE THE NAMES OF YOUR EYELASHES ON EACH ARROW!

⑨

HOW TO CHANGE YOUR HAIR COLOR AT WILL.

POOF!

① Hair color is determined by the mood of your soul. Changing your soul's mood is easier than it sounds.

② The tiniest existential thought will alter the mood of your soul.

③ Untrained soul-mood-changers may end up with a truly horrific hair color. (Think gray-green with a tinge of urinal-yellow.)

④ This skill is worth years of trials and tribulations. Just think, you can now match your hair color to your outfit!

HOW TO BUY SHOES.

1 First of all, it really is true, true beyond belief: You can never have enough shoes. Buy with great abandon. Don't let anyone hold you back.

2 Squeeze your foot into any shoe it will fit into. Squeeze and never let go.

3 Shopping for shoes is akin to boiling cabbage: It is not for the fainthearted.

4 No, it is not ridiculous to dedicate an entire room to your shoe collection.

! ! ! ! ! ! ! ! ! ! !

DRAW YOUR DREAM SHOE COLLECTION ABOVE!!

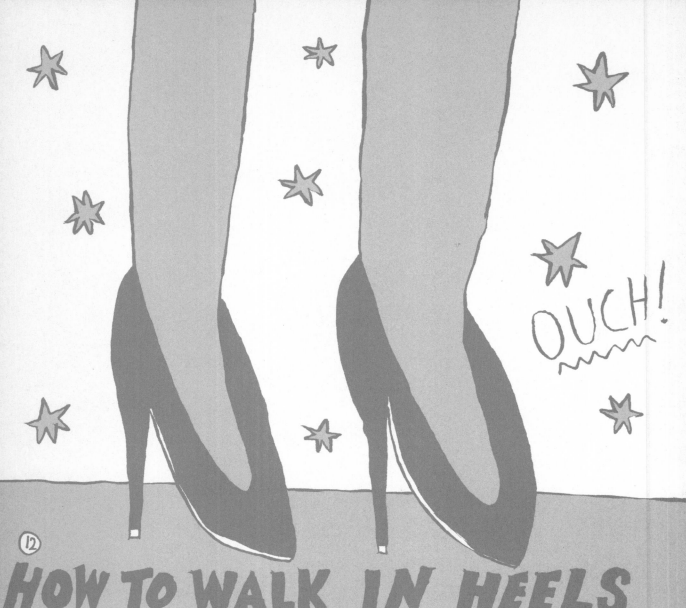

HOW TO WALK IN HEELS.

1. Surgically remove your brain.
2. Begin to take comfort in excruciating pain.
3. Find a focus point (ex: That man's bald spot). This will reduce chances of toppling over by 50%.
4. Never multitask and always carry a wand.

HEELS VS. NO HEELS TIMETABLE

Time yourself doing different activities — once wearing heels and once wearing normal shoes. At the end, compare, and question why you ever decided to purchase heels in the first place. REMEMBER: TIME = MONEY!

ACTIVITY	TIME WITH HEELS	TIME WITHOUT HEELS	DESCRIBE YOUR MOOD AFTER EACH ACTIVITY

HOW TO START A LIP BALM COLLECTION.

(1/100th of the) collection.

1. Lip balm (aka Balm of the Lip) is a rare species of balm that many women and men covet.

2. Create a shrine to the lip balm god in your bedroom. Scatter the corpses of old lipsticks along the bottom. (Lipstick is the sworn mortal enemy of lip balm.)

MWAH!

3. Get lip balm pockets tailored into all your clothes.

4. To keep all your lip balms happy, and to avoid lip balm jealousy, be sure to use each one equally.

BALM ME, BABY!

BEST OF THE BALMS

DRAW YOUR FIRST, SECOND, AND THIRD FAVORITE LIP BALMS ON THE PODIUM BELOW.

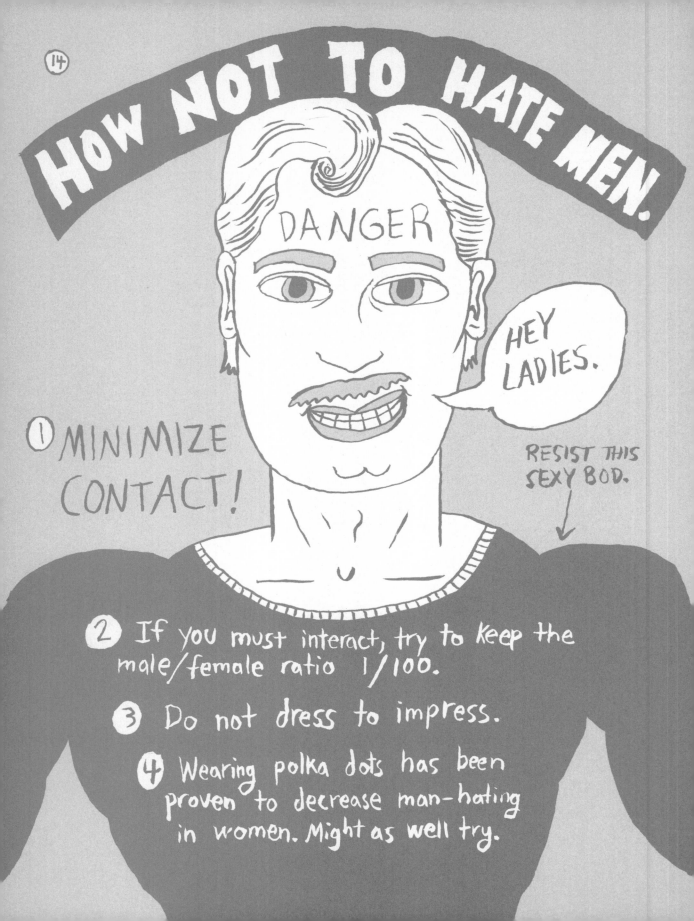

DRAW YOUR FAVORITE AND LEAST FAVORITE MEN BELOW. FEEL FREE TO ADD DESCRIPTIONS. EXPRESS YOURSELF!

HOW TO CHANNEL YOUR INNER HIPPIE.

1. Everyone has a tiny hippie inside them. They usually hide between your fibula and tibia.

2. Hippies can be teased out of hiding with the promise of multigrain bread.

3. If you feel yourself getting really tense and stressed, let your inner hippie take the wheel. (But not literally... hippies aren't known for their driving skills.)

4. Hippies looooovvvveee Scrabble. Get a game going and just wait to see who joins the party.

LOVE ❀ PEACE

TEST OUT YOUR PERCEPTION OF REALITY WITH THIS
HANDY OBSERVATIONAL TEST. SEE HOW DIFFERENT YOU
FEEL IN EVERYDAY SITUATIONS EITHER AS YOURSELF OR
AS A HIPPIE.

SITUATION	YOURSELF	HIPPIE VERSION OF YOU
Checking your emails		
Riding a bicycle		
Talking to your parents		
Eating ice cream		
Doing your makeup		
Cutting your fingernails		
Watching TV		

HOW TO BREW THE

BEST COFFEE EVER

LOVE UR CUP O' JOE

MOST PERFECT CUP OF COFFEE.

1 Realize and accept that brewing coffee is your true calling. Internalize.

2 Coffee beans are unique and individual, just like human beings. Treat them as such.

3 Start a fan club. No one will love your coffee unless other people already love your coffee.

4 Soak your body in tepid water along with your favorite coffee beans.

Coffee Dreams

Everyone dreams about the perfect cup of coffee. Below, write a mini romantic novel starring the coffee of your dreams. Make it hot and steamy!

HOW TO FALL ASLEEP ON THE BUS AND MISS YOUR STOP.

1. Create a playlist specifically tailored to lull your little brain cells into a deep slumber.

2. Sit next to someone who will provide a pillow-like cushion. (This is easier in the wintertime.)

3. Find your "special seat" on the bus that helps you fall asleep. (If someone takes your seat, make them feel VERY uncomfortable.)

4. Drink a sippy cupful of warm milk. Ignore the stares; everyone is just jealous.

SLEEP-INDUCING SENTENCES

WRITE SOME OF THE MOST BORING SENTENCES YOU HAVE EVER READ IN YOUR ENTIRE LIFE BELOW.

1

2

3

4 I was debating between buying the long-hair woven carpet in beige and the fine, short-hair tapestry with tribal geometric patterns.

5

6

7

8

9

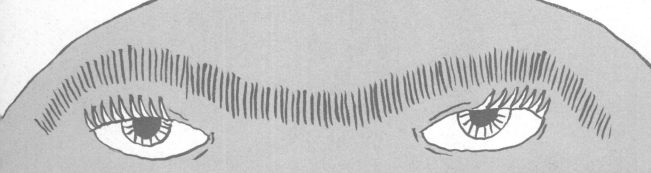

HOW TO GROW A UNIBROW.

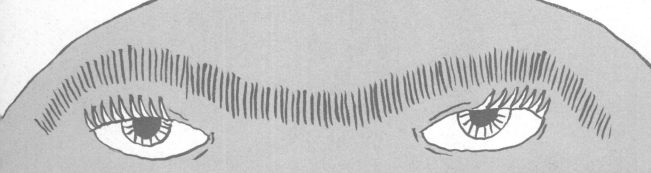

1 Stroke and caress your each and every eyebrow hair follicle.

2 Encourage your eyebrow hairs to start having babies.

3 Write a love letter to the eyebrow god. Beg for an abundant and fruitful unibrow, Amen.

4 Allow your unibrow to pick what to watch on TV every now and then.

HOW TO WALK ELEGANTLY.

1. To walk elegantly you must have perfect posture. To have perfect posture you must subsist on a diet of tender broccoli rabe.

2. Elegance is learned, not bred. The rich have no advantage here!

3. Elegance's mortal enemy is laughter. Only the highest echelon of elegant folks can laugh and maintain elegance.

4. Canasta is the number one game among elegant people.

HOW TO FIGURE OUT THE MEANING OF LIFE

21

① Figuring out the meaning of life might actually be the meaning of life.

② Try not to get discouraged. Be sure to eat lots of snacks.

③ The meaning of life can hide in all sorts of places. It's often found in cereal boxes.

④ Once you figure it out, be sure to impose your beliefs on everyone you come across.

A megaphone really helps!

FIND OUT FOR YOURSELF!

TEST OUT A FEW OF YOUR HYPOTHESES AND FIND THE TRUE MEANING OF LIFE!

Theory #1:

TRUE ☐   FALSE ☐

Theory #2:

TRUE ☐   FALSE ☐

Theory #3:

TRUE ☐   FALSE ☐

HOW TO TRANSFORM INTO A FISH.

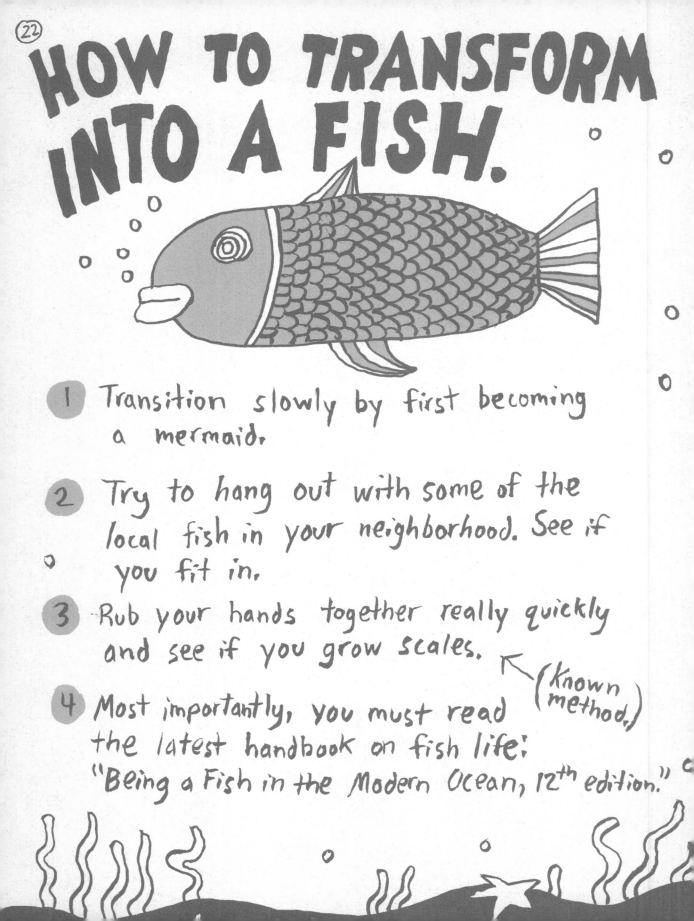

1. Transition slowly by first becoming a mermaid.

2. Try to hang out with some of the local fish in your neighborhood. See if you fit in.

3. Rub your hands together really quickly and see if you grow scales. ← (known method.)

4. Most importantly, you must read the latest handbook on fish life: "Being a Fish in the Modern Ocean, 12th edition."

HOW WOULD YOU LOOK IF YOU WERE A FISH? DRAW IT BELOW!

DRAW A FEW OF YOUR FISHY FRIENDS TOO!!

HOW TO APPRECIATE JAZZ MUSIC.
1 Make that face. You know which face I'm talking about.
2 Put a little bounce in your every step.
3 Speak in a syncopated rhythm. No, PEOPLE will NOT think YOU'RE strange.
4 Doobie doobie doo. Zap bap a doo beep! BOP!

JAZZ IS ALL ABOUT IMPROVISATION AND SELF-EXPRESSION. REACT TO THE OBJECTS ON THIS PAGE EITHER THROUGH DRAWING OR WRITING!

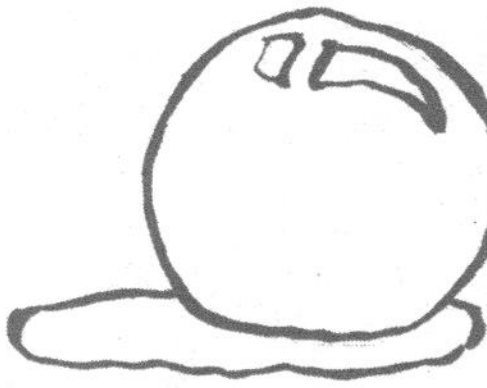

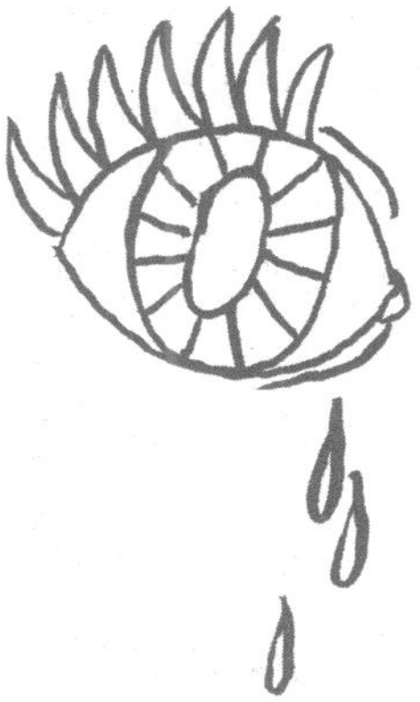

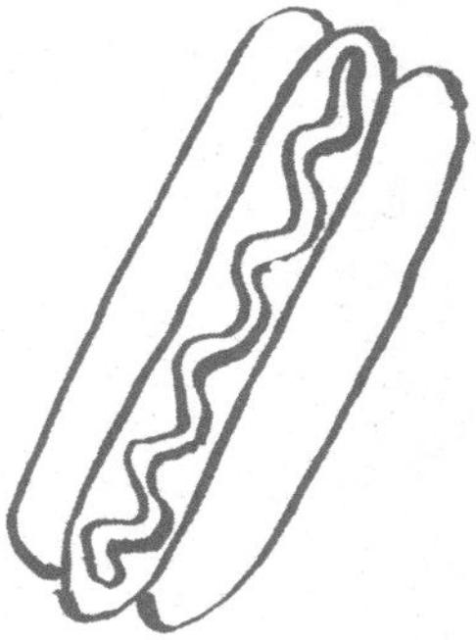

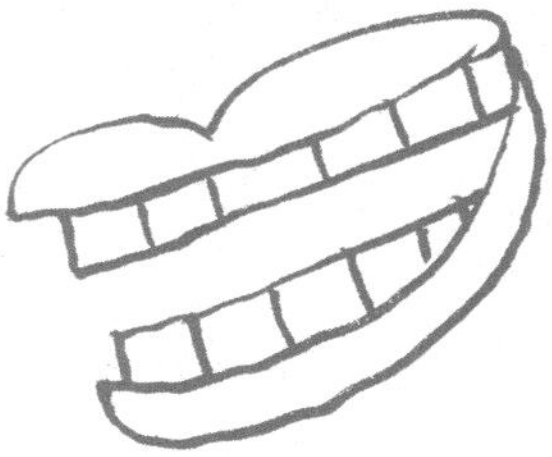

THIS IS ART!!

HOW TO MAKE SMALL TALK. BLAH BLAH BLAH

BLAH BLAH BLAH BLAH BLAH BLAH BLAH

1 Only open your mouth a little bit. This way only small thoughts escape.

2 Laugh casually every five minutes or so. This keeps the conversation light and lively.

3 Lima beans have been known to assist in making small talk.

4 The cleaner your body, the better the conversation.

FUN FACT: Tall people are terrible small talkers. How bizarre!

BLAH BLAH BLAH BLAH BLAH BLAH BLAH BLAH BLAH BLAH

QUICK! RESPOND TO THESE MUNDANE STATEMENTS! YOUR LIFE DEPENDS ON IT!
What's going on with this weather?
Guess it's Monday again, huh?
How was your weekend?
How was your lunch?
What a day!

HOW TO WEAR PLAID.

1 It's not just for the boys, girlies.

Plaid is so non-gender conforming.

2 Wear it on days when you feel a bit sheepish.

Let the world be your oyster!

3 Plaid on plaid on plaid! Mix and match those patterns!

4 Magical powers have been granted to proud plaid wearers of olden days.

DESIGN YOUR OWN SWATCHES
OF PLAID!

HOW TO BE A SOCIAL BUTTERFLY.

① First you must ask yourself: "Do you really want to be a social butterfly?"

② As a high-ranking social butterfly myself, all you really need to know is that you should become my best friend (aka my servant).

③ Being a social butterfly isn't for everyone. It's exhausting and the small-minded simply can't handle it.

④ Higher education preferred. PhDs or better.

DESIGN YOUR SOCIAL BUTTERFLY CROWN!
EVERY QUEEN NEEDS A CROWN!

AAAND YOUR WAND!
YOU MUST HAVE A WAND TO POINT AT THE
UNDERLINGS TO DO YOUR BIDDING!

HOW TO BE A HERMIT.

DO NOT DISTURB.

1 Becoming a hermit can happen overnight. Sleep the wrong way and next morning you will wake up a hermit.

2 If you find yourself growing sick of humanity, or the lack thereof, being a hermit might be for you.

3 There is one cardinal rule of hermiting that you must follow always! Never talk to people.

4 Home is where the hermit is, so be sure to keep it clean and smelling fresh. No one likes a smelly hermit.

If they know you exist!

A DAY IN THE LIFE OF A HERMIT

ISOLATE YOURSELF FROM THE WORLD FOR ONE DAY.
WRITE ABOUT IT BELOW!

OH SWEET SERENITY!

28

HOW NOT TO HATE THE GIRL NEXT DOOR.

① Jealousy gets you nowhere... unless you are the girl next door.

② Accept that certain people are rich and beautiful and suffer minimally during their lifetime.

③ Remove all windows from your house so you never have to see her.

④ Every month or two, to relieve pent-up anger, leave passive—aggressive notes under her door. (Ex: I hate how you park in the driveway. Get a life!)

EVERYONE HAS A GIRL NEXT DOOR IN THEIR LIFE. DRAW AND DESCRIBE YOURS BELOW.

PORTRAIT (FULL BODY):

STATS:

29

HOW TO BE PERCEIVED AS A GENIUS.

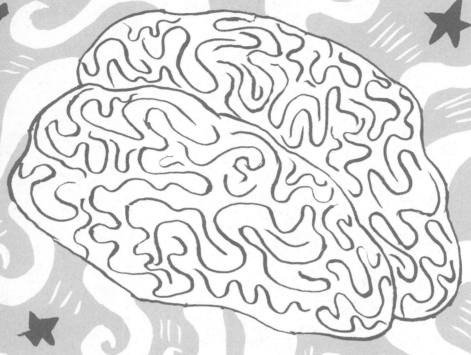

1 Scoff frequently.

2 Carry around large books as accessories.

3 Invite all romantic interests to the library on your first date.

↑ Strategically place bookmarks at least halfway through.

4 Dress either eccentrically or all in black.

㉚ HOW TO FIND THAT PERFECT LITTLE BLACK DRESS.

① Every girl deserves a little black dress ... or does she?

② It wants to be found, but also loves being pursued. Oh, the thrill of the chase!

③ Don't hide your natural pheromones with perfume. To find the perfect little black dress you must attract it with your scent.

④ Once you find it, don't ever let it go. Hold it tight in your arms during long, cold nights.

WHERE DO YOU WANT TO GO WHEN YOU TIME TRAVEL? CHOOSE YOUR TOP THREE PLACES AND WRITE/DRAW THEM BELOW. REMEMBER, ANYTHING IS POSSIBLE!

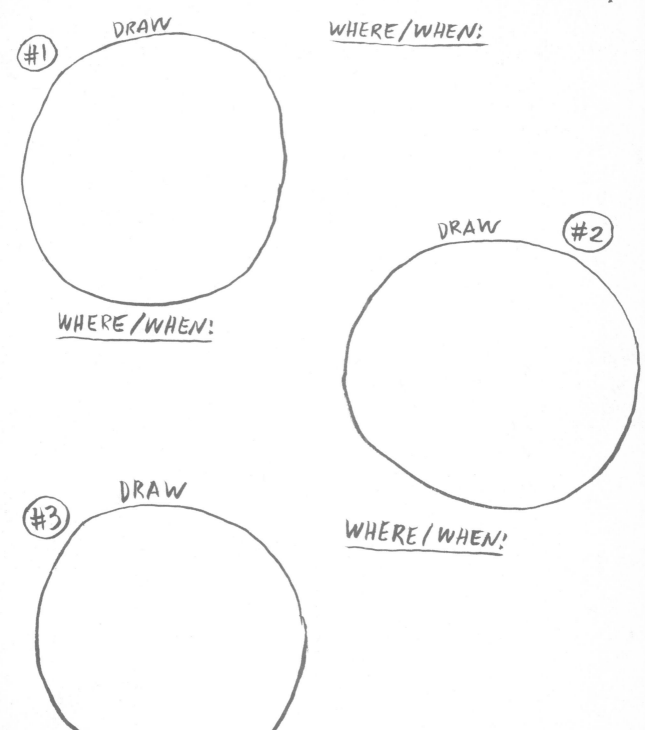

DRAW

#1

WHERE/WHEN:

WHERE/WHEN:

DRAW

#2

WHERE/WHEN:

DRAW

#3

♥ LOVE CHART ♥ ♥ ♥ ♥ ♥ ♥

EVERYONE HAS GOOD QUALITIES, EVEN REALLY SMELLY PEOPLE. FIND A GOOD QUALITY IN EVERYONE YOU KNOW.

PERSON	GOOD QUALITY

33

WWW.HOW TO BECOME A SLAVE TO THE INTERNET.COM.

WORST WEBSITE EVER

www.worstwebsiteever.com

HOME
FAMILY PHOTOS
LIFE STORY
MY BEAUTIFUL FACE
CONTACT
SEND MONEY

1 It's too late, you already are.

2 Reject your physical being and embrace the "realities" of the web.

3 Run into each other's arms, hug, cry, dry each other's tears, and never let go.

4 I now pronounce you Internet and slave.

Type email here to subscribe to our newsletter.
© FOR ALL ETERNITY.

DESIGN YOUR OWN WEBSITE!!!

34

HOW TO MAKE THE MOST OF A VISIT TO YOUR GRANDMA'S.

1. Chat with your grandma beforehand and work out a schedule so you both know what to expect.

2. Keep the conversation light and avoid intergenerational drama.

3. If things start to get intense, maybe take an extended bathroom break. Give grandma some personal time and maybe catch up on your emails.

4. Whatever you do, never turn down food.

ASK YOUR GRANDMA IF YOU CAN LOOK AT HER OLD
PHOTOS, THEN DRAW THEM BELOW.
ADD FUNNY CAPTIONS.

HOW TO MAKE YOUR HAIR GROW QUICKER THAN USUAL.

1 Sing to your hair every night. Motivational pop-rock songs work best.

2 Focus on reading novels that feature heroines with gloriously long locks.

3 Channel hair envy into hair growth. Envy can feed those little follicles.

4 Tousle your hair enthusiastically. (REPEAT 100 TIMES.)

DRAW SOME OF THE PEOPLE WHOSE HAIR YOU
ARE ENVIOUS OF. WE'VE GOT YOU STARTED!!

ELVIS

36

HOW TO PRETEND YOU REALLY LIKE SOMEONE.

arm's length distance

1 Shower them with gifts until they become buried underneath a pile of them.

2 Compliment them on superficial things. ("You've got good breath!" or "Your hair looks clean!")

3 Sit next to them during class, but minimize conversation. ("Sorry, I need silence to focus.")

4 Smile as you pass them in the hallway. They probably won't notice the dead look behind your eyes.

MAKE - BELIEVE!

DRAW TWO PEOPLE BELOW WHO YOU COULD SEE YOURSELF
PRETENDING TO LIKE. WRITE WHY.

37

HOW TO PRETEND YOU ARE REALLY INTERESTED IN SOMETHING SOMEONE IS TALKING ABOUT.

I'M ALL EARS!

① Constantly nod and maintain eye contact with their right eyeball.

② Have a set of generic phrases that you can call upon if you need to respond.

↑ Ex: "Mmmhmmm."

③ Sync your circadian rhythm with their circadian rhythm.

④ Take notes. Dispose of them before bed.

TAKE NOTES HERE THE NEXT TIME YOU'RE BORED.

HOW TO BE REAL.

CERTIFIED REAL SEAL

1 Know it. Own it. Make it 100% you, baby.

2 Soak your body and mind in YOU. Let your pores exude your 100% real natural pheromones. *SNIFF*

3 Change your middle name to something mind-altering...something so...YOU.

4 There is no time like the present, so PRESENT yourself like a beautiful present.

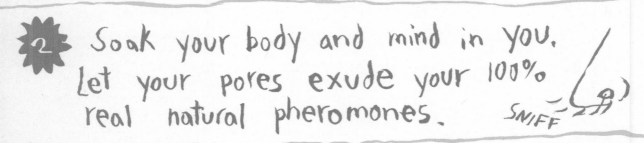

Yeah, I'm me and only me, 100% me, 100% of the TIME.

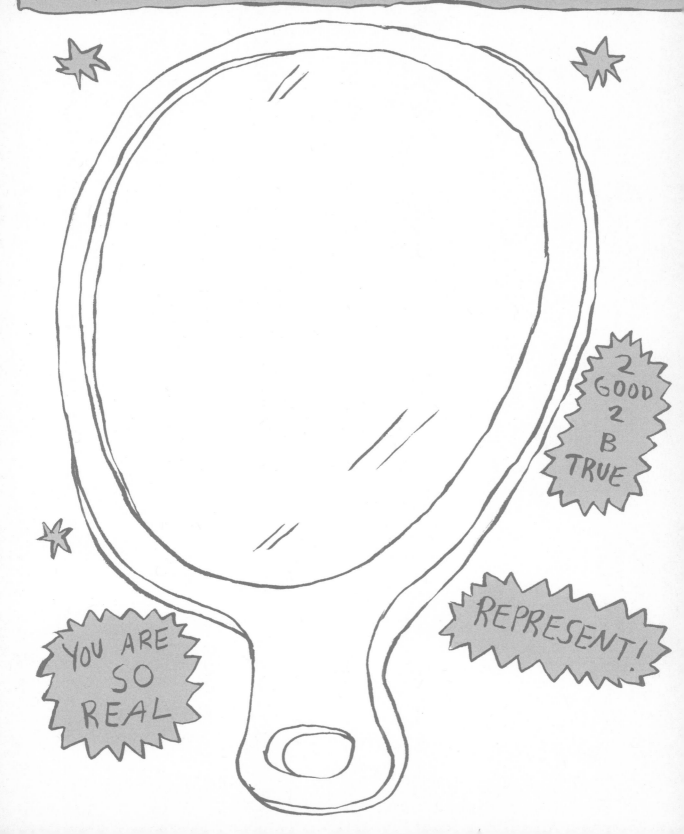

HOW TO SING YOURSELF TO SLEEP.

1 Pick a song that tickles your subconscious' fancy. Enya, anyone?

2 It's not so much "singing yourself to sleep," as it is "humming yourself to sleep." A fine distinction, but an important one.

3 Studies have shown that those who wear brightly colored socks have a greater chance of singing themselves to sleep.

4 While singing, pretend you are at a rummage sale and you have just fallen into a box of musty overcoats from circa 1983. Sleep is on its way, baby, it's on its way.

HOW TO BE AN ARTIST.

THIS IS ART

1. Find a focus and REALLY, really focus on it. (Ex: Blue paintings of rare earthworm species.)

2. You must simultaneously be eccentric yet able to socialize with wealthy people.

3. Be sure to live in the artsy part of town. There is no such thing as an artist from the suburbs.

4. Choose friends who will add to your collectibility appeal. You need people at your openings who will make you and your paintings look better.

HOW TO BE FAKE.

UNCERTIFIED SHINY STICKER

 1 False eyelashes, false promises, broken hearts. Pick your poison.

 2 Was that you...or your evil twin? Or your shadow soul spirit incarnate?

3 Lurking in the moonlight, I see your black soul through your beady little eyes. Idol worshipper! Idol worshipper!

 4 Rub your hands together, child.

GOD#5

DRAW YOUR FAKE ID.

FRONT

BACK

READ THE MINDS OF A FEW OF YOUR LOVED ONES...AND A FEW OF YOUR MORTAL ENEMIES.

PERSON 1:

PERSON 2:

PERSON 3:

PERSON 4:

PERSON 5:

PERSON 6:

43

HOW TO SPREAD WORLD PEACE.

1 Use a butter knife and spread a nice even coat all over the globe.

2 Calmly remind everyone how important it is to remain calm.

↳ Global yoga classes, anyone?

3 One day we will all be wearing adult diapers... so... CHILL OUT!!!

4 Starting wars is SO last season.

l agree to spread world peace.

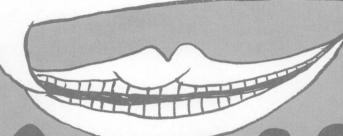

HOW TO SPEAK ONLY IN METAPHORS.

1 Eat a healthy breakfast every morning. Metaphors run on protein and fiber.

2 Throw your brain into the jail cell of your mind. Only let the metaphors walk free.

3 Surround yourself with friends who also subscribe to the metaphor lifestyle.

4 Don't expect everyone to accept and understand you. They may not be as evolved as you are.

YOUR LIFE IS ONE GIANT METAPHOR. WRITE
DOWN EIGHT MAJOR LIFE EVENTS, THEN FIND A
METAPHOR THAT SUMMARIZES THEM ALL.

THIS
METAPHOR

HOW TO PRETEND YOU ARE A FOREIGNER.

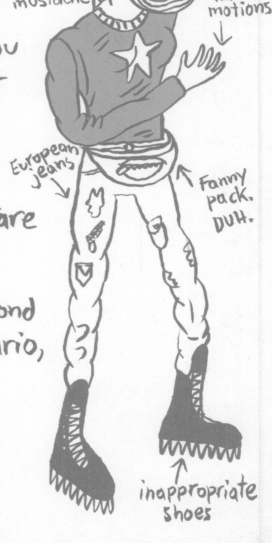

beret

fake mustache

dramatic hand motions

European jeans

Fanny pack. DUH.

inappropriate shoes

1. Be sure to keep your children out late. If you are a child, stay out past your bedtime.

2. Walk slower than the average pace of your city/town. Stop and stare frequently.

3. If possible, learn a second language. Worse case scenario, speak broken English.

4. Wear weather-inappropriate clothing.

↑
sneakers with
heels

DRAW YOUR "BEARY" BEST FRIEND.
YOUR BROTHER FROM ANOTHER HAIRIER MOTHER.

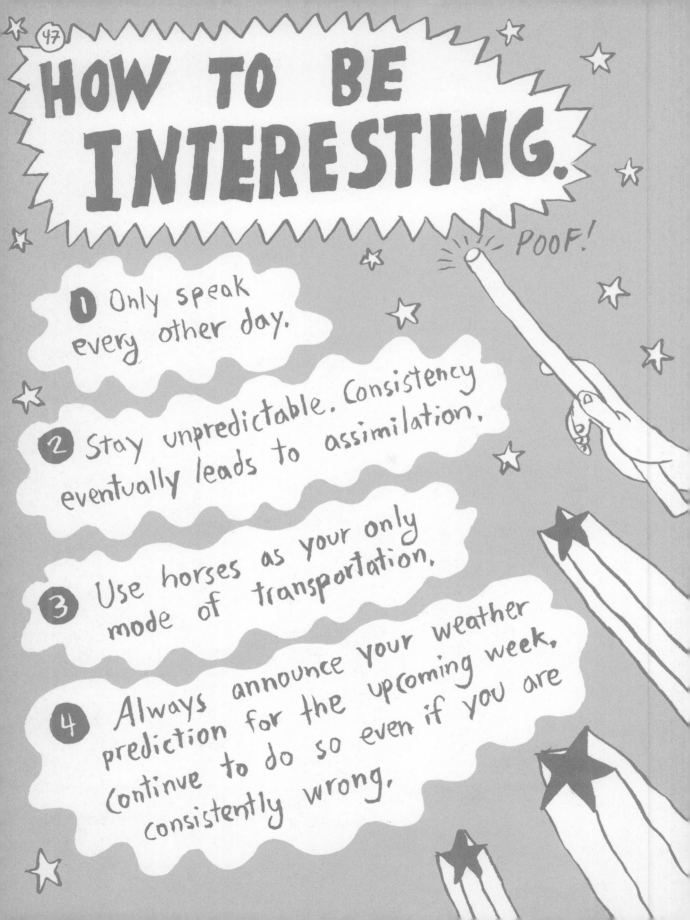

HOW TO BE INTERESTING.

POOF!

1 Only speak every other day.

2 Stay unpredictable. Consistency eventually leads to assimilation.

3 Use horses as your only mode of transportation.

4 Always announce your weather prediction for the upcoming week. Continue to do so even if you are consistently wrong.

KEEP TRACK OF THE THINGS YOU DO TO BECOME MORE INTERESTING. KEEP IT SPICY!

INTERESTING LOG #1!

INTERESTING LOG #2!

INTERESTING LOG #3!

① Buy a really awesome spy hat.

② Invent your own code language for communicating with the mother country.

③ Take mental notes with your eyes. It's all about being observant yet casual.

④ If ever questioned, tell people you had a nomadic youth and don't remember much of it.

AS A SPY, YOU'VE GOT TO KEEP YOUR STORY STRAIGHT.
WRITE A SHORT BIO BELOW.

BIO:

COUNTRY OF ORIGIN: BIRTHDAY:

SPY GADGETS: DRAW YOUR TRUSTY TOOLS BELOW.

← ICE POP
ANTIDOTE
(counterarts all)
poisons

← FAKE
MOLE

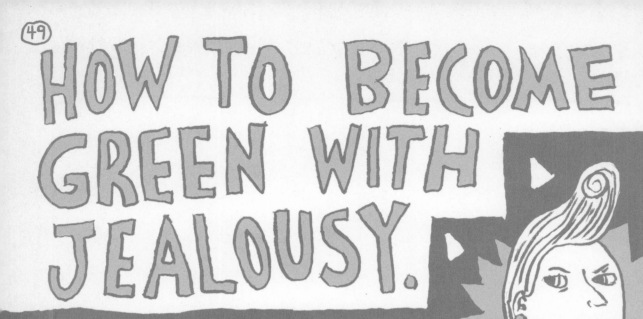

HOW TO BECOME GREEN WITH JEALOUSY.

1. "Oooooooh... how dare she? HOW COULD SHE?! Why, if I..." ← REPEAT OVER AND OVER IN YOUR HEAD.

2. Try and melt into the greenest of grasses. Then reconstitute into a greener version of yourself.

↖ Ideally use your neighbor's lawn. (sorry city-dwellers.)

3. Cook all your meals with green food coloring.

4. Jealousy is the gateway to full-blown paranoia. You've got to start somewhere!

50

HOW TO CONTROL THE WEATHER.

1 Get on Mother Nature's good side. (Hint: Double-shot chai latte.)

2 Offer to babysit her children. Accept that there will be some natural disasters.

3 If you don't have one already, you better start developing a god complex.

4 Remember, the weather is fickle, just like your unruly cowlick. But even fickle things can be controlled with the right hair product.

51

HOW TO BE A WALLFLOWER.

1 Being a wallflower is actually quite important. Who will decorate the wall if not you?

2 Visit the venue ahead of time so that you know the wall color. Coordinate your outfit to match.

3 Plan some solitary activities you can do while near a wall. (Ex: One-person tennis, wall squats, hand stands, etc.)

4 Stay away from other wallflowers. They are not to be trusted.

The Wallflower Diaries

WRITE YOUR OBSERVATIONS WHILE BEING A WALLFLOWER. KEEP THINGS SNARKY AND DISMAL.

52

HOW TO SAVE MONEY.

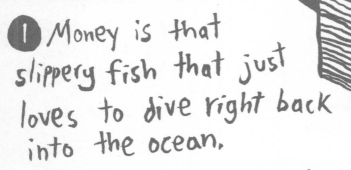

1 Money is that slippery fish that just loves to dive right back into the ocean.

2 You will never have to save money if you don't have money. If that's the case, offer to help save other people's money! (Much less stressful.)

3 "Don't count your money-chickens before they hatch." — that wise old person.

4 No one ever asks money how it feels. Does it really want to be saved? Or are we simply imposing our value system upon it?

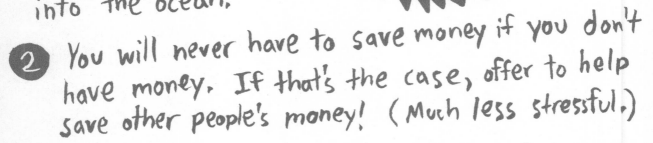

WRITE AN OBITUARY FOR ALL THE GOOD MONEY THAT JUST COULD NOT BE SAVED. IT MAY BE GONE, BUT IT WILL NEVER BE FORGOTTEN.

R.I.P.

53

HOW TO BE A HEALTH NUT.

1. Get crazy with your nutty self.

2. Believe it or not, health nuts do not eat nuts.

3. Always dress in activewear. If possible, maintain an attractive level of perspiration.

4. Keep your kale chips close and your protein shakes closer.

DRAW SOME OF YOUR FAVORITE HEALTH SNACKS! WRITE WHY YOU LOVE THEM TOO!

BABY CARROTS!
Just like eating
babies!

RADISHES!
They are so
red and white!

54

HOW TO BECOME A BODYBUILDER.

1 Being a bodybuilder is more than a hobby, it's a national pastime.

2 By simply spending time at the gym your muscles will begin to grow.

3 Grunting loudly while lifting weights quadruples muscle growth.

4 Spend long, hard minutes staring at yourself in the mirror. The more minutes you stare, the more irresistible your body becomes.

FOREVER STRONG!

HOW TO COLLECT CATS.

PURRRRRRR

—MEOW!

1. Believe it or not, whether you will become a cat collector or not is genetically determined. (It is passed down through the paternal side.)

2. Cat collectors are most commonly found in the Midwest.

3. Make cats feel right at home by wearing argyle sweaters and wool socks.

4. Buy the annual "Guide to Professional Cat Collecting: Understanding Every Meow."

DRAW A CAT TO MATCH EACH NAME.

PICKLES

MR TOM

BETTY

VANILLA BEAN

LEO TOLSTOY

SUN BABY

56

HOW TO RIDE A HORSE.

1 Brush your horse's mane and whisper in their ear that you love them,

2 Make sure your horse matches you in attractiveness.

3 Promise them you'll never drive a car ever again. (Never, ever, ever!!)

4 Prepare by reading every romantic novel that has a horse on the cover.

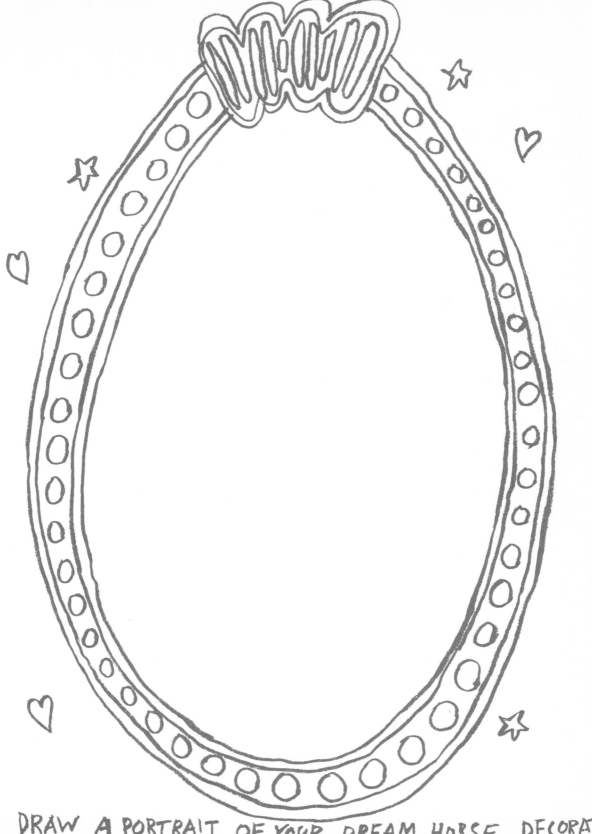

DRAW A PORTRAIT OF YOUR DREAM HORSE, DECORATE
ALL AROUND THE BORDER.

HOW TO TURN YOUR LIFE INTO A SOAP OPERA.

57

1 The world is your mortal enemy AND your bestest friend simultaneously. Act accordingly.

2 Change romantic partners every two weeks. Make sure they all know each other.

3 Spend equal amounts of time crying and applying makeup.

4 Try always to look devastated, electrified, and confused.

DRAMA!!!

REGULAR ACTIVITY	SOAP-OPERA VERSION

SPICE UP YOUR EVERYDAY ACTIVITIES! WRITE YOUR ALTERNATIVES ON THIS CHART. KEEP IT DRAMATIC!!

HOW TO BE CLAIRVOYANT.

58

① Announce to everyone, very loudly, that you are clairvoyant.

② Instead of a winter coat, wear a velvet robe during the cold season.

③ When people talk to you, say "mmm HHHmm" with an all-knowing intonation.

④ Though stereotypical, carrying around a crystal ball can help credibility.

WRITE YOUR PREDICTIONS
FOR THE FUTURE HERE.
CHECK BACK IN TEN YEARS.

HOW NOT TO LOSE YOUR MIND IN A CROWDED SUBWAY CAR.

GOD HELP ME!!

① Always carry a reserve tank of oxygen with you.
Fresh air = clear mind.

② Limit outside stimuli by wearing headphones, sunglasses, and a full-body hazmat suit.

③ If you must make eye contact with a stranger, look away quickly and pretend it never happened.

④ Glare at one of the lucky people with a seat. Telepathically convince them to give it to you.

"I swear you WILL give me that seat if it's the last thing I do."

HOW TO BE REALLY AWKWARD.

← awkward period

1. Start every sentence with nervous laughter.

2. Stand either too close for comfort or too far away to be heard.

3. Do that thing where you play with your toenails while maintaining really intense eye contact.

4. Overshare during inopportune moments. (Ex: In an elevator, during long car journeys, etc.)

Well, isn't this empty space on the page a little awkward?

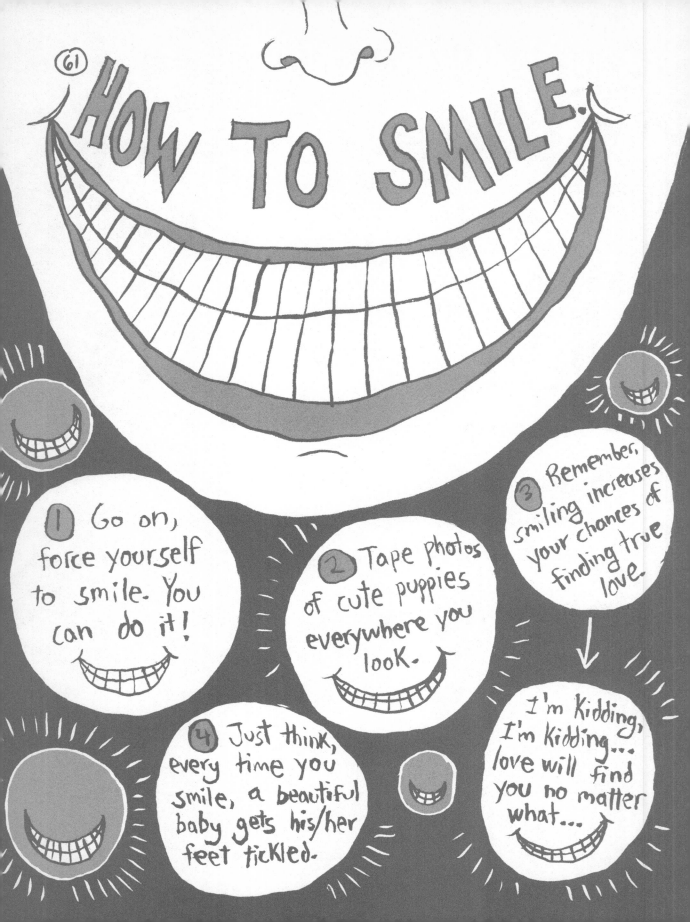

HOW TO COOK EGGS.
2 Crack open your egg at a 45° angle.
1 There is no wrong way to cook an egg.
FALSE
TRUE
3 Rejoice in the juices of egg.
4 Massage the egg, whisper sweet nothings to the egg. LOVE THE EGG!

The Egg Wedding

WHAT HAPPENS IF YOUR EGGS WANT TO GET MARRIED?

PLAN THEIR WEDDING BELOW! SPARE NO DETAIL OR EXPENSE!

YOUR BREAKFAST DEPENDS ON IT!

HOW TO FIND A WAY INTO EVERYONE'S HEART.
THE UNIVERSAL HEART
MASTER KEY
1 Plant the seed of love, then be sure to water it every couple of days.
2 Be so gosh darn ADORABLE!!!
3 Discover each person's particular hobbies, then adopt them only long enough to gain their friendship.
4 Wear only warm colors so as to appear inviting and vivacious. Avoid black at all costs!

HOW TO BE A DRAMA QUEEN.

64

1 Everything is a big deal, "What do you mean there is no ketchup on my frittata?!"

2 Always be on the verge of snapping. Everyone you know and don't know should be on edge when they are near you.

3 Start developing gravitational pull. You need it if you plan on being the center of the universe.

4 Learn to cry on command. You need to garner people's sympathy every now and then.

START GETTING REALLY SELF-RIGHTEOUS! LIST A FEW OF THE THINGS YOU CAN USE TO START DRAMA.

TO BE A DRAMA QUEEN YOU NEED A TINY BLACK HEART. DRAW YOURS!

GET YOUR DRAMA QUEEN FACE READY! DRAW YOURS BELOW.

65

HOW TO HAVE THE MOST *Perfect* HANDWRITING.

⭐ **1** Perfect handwriting is an undervalued skill in this world of ours. And there is nothing more important than perfecting an undervalued skill.

⭐ **2** Chain yourself to a desk and write under the strict supervision of a handwriting master (or Guardian of the Written Word, as they like to call themselves).

⭐ **3** Whistle while you write! It makes the letters come out SO much easier.

⭐ **4** Take yourself very seriously (even while you whistle).

PRACTICE WRITING YOUR NAME PERFECTLY BELOW.

My name is the best!

66

HOW TO LOVE YOUR FEET.

1 Feet deserve as much love as the rest of your body. Treat them well and they will take you where you want to go.

2 The aroma of cinnamon makes any little foot absolutely lose its mind! Rub it down with that special spice every now and then.

3 Yes, feet need to be washed. Nothing screams foot neglect more than dirt between your toes.

4 The more you see your feet, the more you love them. They are social creatures, just like the rest of us. Invite them to the party!

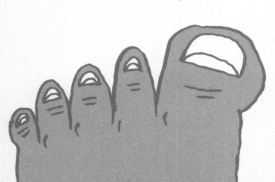

DRAW YOUR FEET'S PORTRAIT BELOW!
GET IN ALL THOSE FOOTY DETAILS.

PEEKABOO!

HOW TO CLIMB REALLY HIGH.

67

1. Despite popular opinion, climbing really high really is for the fainthearted.

2. When you climb really high you get a better perspective on all your problems.
   ↘ "So THAT'S why I can't fit into size four jeans!"

3. The air is cleaner up high. It detoxes your whole circulatory system.

4. Bring multiple GPS devices on your journey upward. This way you will receive varied opinions on the best way to go.

DIARY OF A TREE CLIMBER.

DRAW THE TREES YOU CLIMB,
THEN WRITE THE MOOD YOU WERE IN
WHEN YOU WERE AT THE TOP.

Transcendental

68

HOW TO BE MAGNANIMOUS

This word is really magnanimous.

1. Step one: Learn the definition of magnanimous.

2. Step two: Run with wild antelope and live to tell people about it.

3. Step three: Cut off all your hair and donate it to charity.

4. Step four: Live the rest of your life magnanimously.

← This hand is filled with magnanimous things.

DRAW YOURSELF IN YOUR MOST MAGNANIMOUS OUTFIT.
SURROUNDED BY ANTELOPE.

69

HOW LITERALLY TO BECOME A FIGURE OF SPEECH.

(1) You are not what you seem, and what seems to be may not be real. Really!

I'M WATCHING MY GIRLISH FIGURE... OF SPEECH!

(2) Subsist on a diet of leafy metaphors and scrumptious similies.

(3) Let your imagination hold your brain hostage. Sanity is for those with loose morals.

(4) Remember, figures of speech come in all shapes and sizes.

HOW TO UNDERSTAND POETRY.

BOOK O' POEMS

① Become very familiar with the unfamiliar.

② 'Twas the night before Christmas, ain't that a shame?

this is poetry

③ Get into the habit of wandering around every noun, adjective, verb, and pronoun in your neighborhood. Get to know them REAL good.

④ It is not a question of understanding; it is a question of embodying all that is not understood. Understand?

An Ode to My Body
by
Tell me o' body,
tell me now.

HOW TO START YOUR OWN FAN CLUB.

OMG!!!

sigh

I LOVE YOU!!!

MARRY ME!!!

EEEEEEE EEEEEEEE EEEEEEEE!!

1. Identify your celebrity persona and embody it. Mind, body, and soul.

2. Be elusive and always leave people desiring more.

3. Be the person that everyone loathes and loves. They can't stand you, but want to know everything about you.

4. Sell merchandise with your face on it.

BONUS TIP: Endorse products even if you aren't asked to.

ONCE YOU HAVE A FAN CLUB, THERE IS NO DOUBT THAT DIFFERENT MEDIA OUTLETS WILL WANT TO INTERVIEW YOU. PRACTICE ON THESE QUESTIONS BELOW:

HOW HAS YOUR LIFE CHANGED SINCE YOUR NEWFOUND FAME?

DO YOU DONATE TO ANY CHARITABLE CAUSES?

WHAT'S YOUR FAVORITE COLOR?

WHAT BRAND OF DESIGNER PJS DO YOU WEAR?

WHAT TIME IS IT?

WHAT ARE YOU DOING ON FRIDAY NIGHT?

73

HOW TO MOISTURIZE.

1 Change your birthday so you are a water sign. Water signs always have youthful complexions.

2 Only bathe once a week. Natural oils keep your skin and hair smooth.

3 Never drive over 25 mph. Speed increases the visibility of wrinkles.

4 Creams should be applied from the toes upward.

NEW BIRTHDAY:

NEW ASTROLOGICAL SIGN:

NEW OUTLOOK ON LIFE:

DRAW YOUR MOISTURIZED TOES:

HOW TO BITE YOUR TONGUE.

OUCH!

SILENCE HURTS!

① You should probably bite your tongue more often than not.

② If you feel some rogue words trying to escape from your mouth, have your tongue whip them into submission. Hopefully they will call it a night.

③ Imagine how different history would have been if we had been a people of tongue biters. Fewer wars, fewer gossip magazines...

④ If, by mistake, you say something unfortunate, don't beat yourself up, but please cry yourself to sleep.

DOCUMENT ALL THE INCIDENTS WHEN YOU SHOULD HAVE HELD YOUR TONGUE.

HOW TO BE THOUGHTFUL.

MY MIND IS FILLED WITH SO MANY THOUGHTS.

I AM A THOUGHTFUL THOUGHT.

thoughtfully high-waisted jeans

1. In my opinion, it takes way too much thought to be thoughtful. But if you must, begin with considering the feelings of others.

2. "I am not the center of the universe. I am not the center of the universe. I am not..."

3. Try to be thoughtful in times of least need. It will require less effort on your part.

4. Think as many thoughts as possible. At least a few of them will be thoughtful.

CHARACTER DEVELOPMENT.

IT'S ABOUT TIME YOU DEVELOPED SOME CHARACTER.
COMPLETE THE SENTENCES BELOW THOUGHTFULLY.

I AM THOUGHTFUL WHEN...

I AM THOUGHTLESS WHEN...

I AM MOTIVATED BY...

MY LIMITS ARE...

I CAN'T RESIST...

I LOVE...

I CAN'T STAND...

I AM TORMENTED BY...

I SPEND MOST OF MY TIME...

FINAL THOUGHTS....

76

HOW TO AVOID DOING LAUNDRY.

1 Start a book collection. Store it on top of the laundry machine. (What an economical use of space!)

2 Purchase enough underwear for the year. Nothing else ever really needs to be washed.

3 Own your new body odor. Tell people it's this really expensive new perfume you found online.

4 Take showers with your clothes on. Two-in-one, very time efficient.

KEEP TRACK OF ALL THE CLOTHING YOU WEAR AND DON'T WASH.

Polka-dotted undies.

77

HOW TO GO ON A DATE.

Love is in the air!

1 Getting a date is half the battle. If you've achieved this you have (almost) nothing to worry about.

2 Eating minty chocolates is not the same as brushing your teeth.

3 Try to reveal only one bad quality. A good rule of thumb is one bad quality per date.

Example: "So, tell me, what do you consider to be your worst physical flaw?"

4 Ask invasive questions.

DREAM DATES AND HEARTTHROBS... WE ALL
HAVE THEM! DRAW A FEW OF YOURS BELOW.

78

HOW TO CREATE A MASTERPIECE.

1 There is a masterpiece brewing inside each and every one of us. The trick is to brew it with all the right ingredients.

2 Live in isolation for a few years, then emerge with your masterpiece. Try to get some good PR from local news stations and magazines.

3 Get a lot, A LOT of popular people to go on record proclaiming your genius.

4 Refuse to explain the meaning of your masterpiece to anyone. Whenever asked, just say, "Its meaning has transcended my earthly mind."

CREATING A MASTERPIECE IS A LOT OF PRESSURE. SO, INSTEAD, CREATE YOUR ANTI-MASTERPIECE HERE.

79

HOW TO MELT SOMEONE'S HEART.

♥ 1 Secretly start raising the temperature in the room 5° at a time.

♥ 2 Stare deeply and intensely into their eyes until you can sense their heart starting to beat faster.

♥ 3 Every time you see them, profess your undying love.

♥ 4 Get a restraining order against them, then write a letter explaining how your love is too strong, you fear your heart might burst at the sight of their face.

LAST RESORT →

HOW TO FLY.

1 Let your spirit free. Open the cage you keep it in and throw away the key.

2 Make dramatic arm and hand motions to attract the attention of those around you, then blast off!

3 Fly with other flocks of humans for safety during long journeys.

4 Keep legumes out of your diet. They can affect your sense of direction.

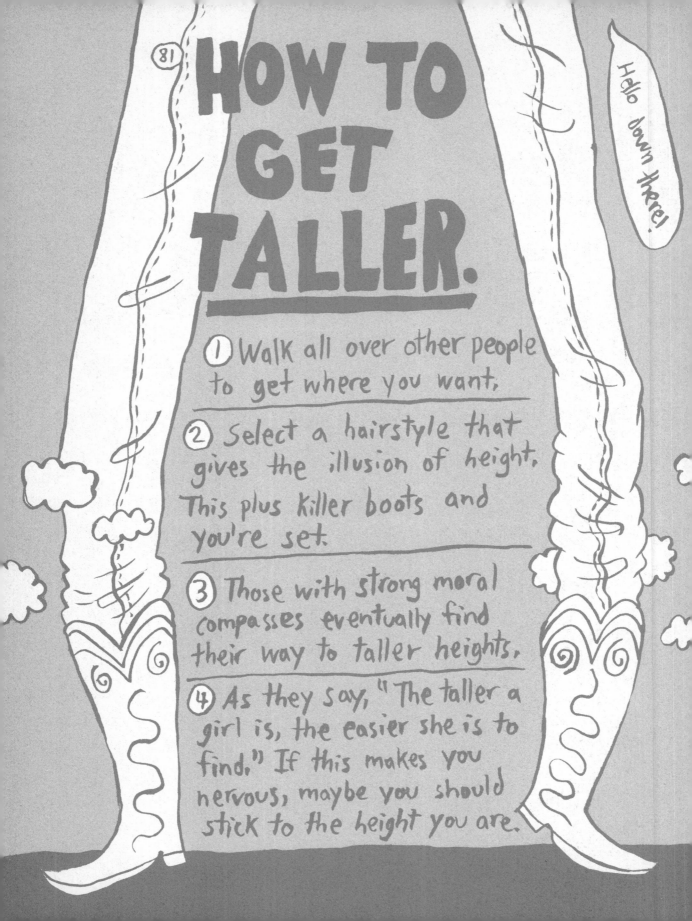

HOW WOULD YOUR LIFE CHANGE IF YOU WERE TALLER? EXPLAIN.

NAME SOME PEOPLE YOU WISH WERE SHORTER.

DRAW YOUR FAVORITE "GET-TALL" BOOTS.

DRAW YOUR FAVORITE TALL PERSON.

READY, SET, GET TALL!

82

HOW TO PLAY THE PIANO.

GENIUS AT WORK. DO NOT DISTURB.

1. Get your fingers programed with the most up-to-date piano-playing software.

2. Be sure to get enough protein in your diet. Those little fingers of yours need strength and endurance.

3. Start a piano-playing-prodigy club with the other local piano prodigies.
   ↳ Make PPP club badges (Piano-Playing Prodigy).

PPP WE R THE BEST

4. Jiggle those black and whites! (Jiggle them real good.)

DESIGN PPP BADGES FOR ALL THE DIFFERENT CLUB DIVISIONS ALL OVER THE WORLD.

SAN FRANCISCO

NEW YORK

LONDON

SOUTH AFRICA

VENEZUELA

ISRAEL

CHINA

RUSSIA

83

HOW TO APPRECIATE WHAT YOU HAVE.

→

1 Constantly stare at your few possessions. They are beautiful and lovely.

2 Name each one of the objects you own. Speak to them as though they are people.

3 Only befriend people who own fewer things than you.

I'm sorry, you're just not my type...

4 Lick everything. Leave your scent on each and every item. Mark your TERRITORY!

EMPTY YOUR POCKETS AND PURSE. DRAW EVERY SINGLE ITEM BELOW. EVEN THE LINT AND OLD RECEIPTS!

84

HOW TO BE A POLITICAL PERSON.

VOTE 4 THIS PERSON

① You can either be a political person or a POLITICAL person. Choose wisely.

② If you decide to become political, don't allow it to consume any more than 10% of your life. Any more than 10% and you might turn into a political animal!

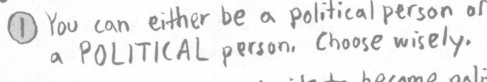

NO, VOTE 4 THAT PERSON

③ Political thoughts are known to have caused violent reactions and sometimes headaches and high fevers.

④ When running in political circles, be sure to bring your own towel. (No one will let you borrow theirs.)

85

HOW TO KEEP UP WITH THE NEWS

THE NEWS

OH, THE HORROR!

"I CAN'T FEEL MY FEELINGS" ANYMORE.

"LIFE IS TRULY TERRIBLE"

AND NOT GET DEPRESSED.

1 Only read the weather report and the horoscopes.

2 Keep telling yourself that this is only a dream...everyone is going to wake up soon, right? Right?!

3 Turn to the Bible and the word of God. Let that be your only source of news and you'll be all good.

4 Stick to the really local news, like the news that only exists within your mind.

THIS PAGE WILL RESTORE YOUR FAITH IN HUMANITY.

Write down all the news you read that makes you happy. Return to this page during dark times.

LOVE
IS
ALL!

86

HOW TO LIVE A BOHEMIAN LIFESTYLE.

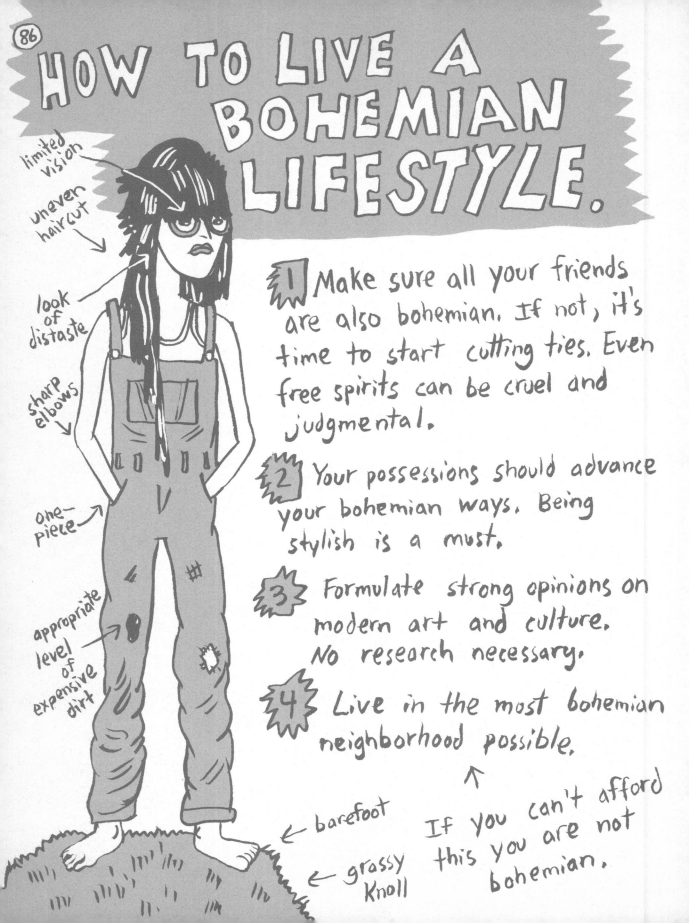

limited vision

uneven haircut

look of distaste

sharp elbows

one-piece

appropriate level of expensive dirt

1 Make sure all your friends are also bohemian. If not, it's time to start cutting ties. Even free spirits can be cruel and judgmental.

2 Your possessions should advance your bohemian ways. Being stylish is a must.

3 Formulate strong opinions on modern art and culture. No research necessary.

4 Live in the most bohemian neighborhood possible.

← barefoot

← grassy knoll

If you can't afford this you are not bohemian.

My Bohemian Diary. WRITE AN ENTRY!

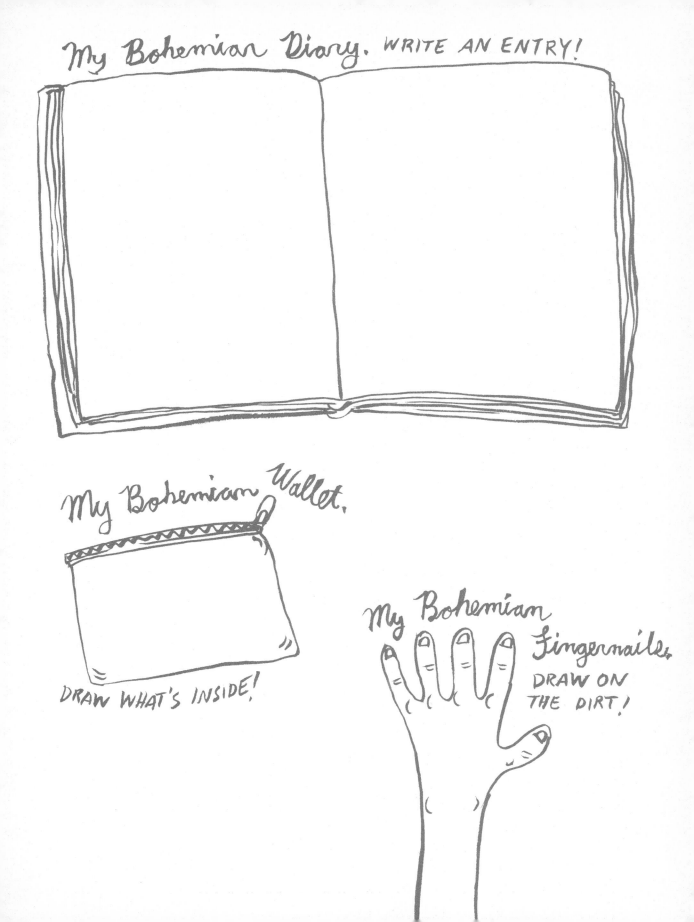

My Bohemian Wallet.

DRAW WHAT'S INSIDE!

My Bohemian Fingernails DRAW ON THE DIRT!

87

HOW TO DEAL WITH MONEY.

1. Money has a pretty nasty attitude, so be sure to put it in its place every once in a while.

2. Tell that money to put its money where its mouth is.

3. A light spanking across the bottom never did any harm.

4. Expect headaches and occasional cramps. Serious side effects are not commonly reported, but consult your doctor before dealing with large amounts of money.

PROFESSIONAL MONEY ALL-STAR

DRAW YOUR FAVORITE MONEY-
ATHLETE, INCLUDE UNIFORM,
TATTOOS, CURRENCY TYPE, AND
MEDALS/TROPHIES.

MONEY-ATHLETE BIO'

HOW TO BECOME REALLY FLEXIBLE.

1. Start each morning with a bowl of fiber-rich cereal.

2. Read up on the lives of really inspirational rubber bands.

3. Befriend really difficult people and cave into all their requests.

4. Reach for the stars... literally.
(I know, I know...we just couldn't resist.)

WRITE AN INSPIRATIONAL QUOTE INSIDE EACH RUBBER BAND.

REMEMBER THESE DURING TIMES OF INFLEXIBILITY.

HOW TO TIE THE MOST PERFECT PONYTAIL.

OMG! SO PERFECT!

LUVIN' IT!

1 The perfect ponytail starts with a perfectly shaped skull. (Sorry for those without this. Tough luck.)

2 Only use hair ties made of 100% Scandinavian woven textiles.

3 Generally, tying your hair between the hours of 9–10 a.m. provides the best results.

4 Always show off your pony. Make the other girls JEALOUS!

HOW TO BE A PICKY EATER.

① Only eat food from one food group (two at most). Prepare to rationalize this decision when confronted.

② Go out with friends, say you'll eat "anything," then complain throughout the meal that there is nothing to eat.

③ Deconstruct every meal and only eat one of its ingredients.

④ Just a heads up, being a picky eater is probably the most unattractive quality a person could ever have.

↑ UNWANTED BROCCOLI

↑ SAD PEAS

HOW TO ENJOY RUNNING.

1. Find less enjoyment in everything else and all of a sudden running might seem somewhat tolerable.

2. Spend a lot of money on running shoes and clothing.

3. Constantly remind yourself that running allows you to become the beautiful person you want to be.

4. Become a runner with a corporate sponsor. More money = less pain.

THE RUNNING CHRONICLES

DOCUMENT BELOW EXACTLY HOW YOU FEEL RIGHT WHEN YOU COMPLETE YOUR RUN, DETAILS PLEASE!!

DAY 1

DAY 2

DAY 3

DAY 4

DAY 5

DAY 6

HOW TO WRITE A LOVE LETTER.

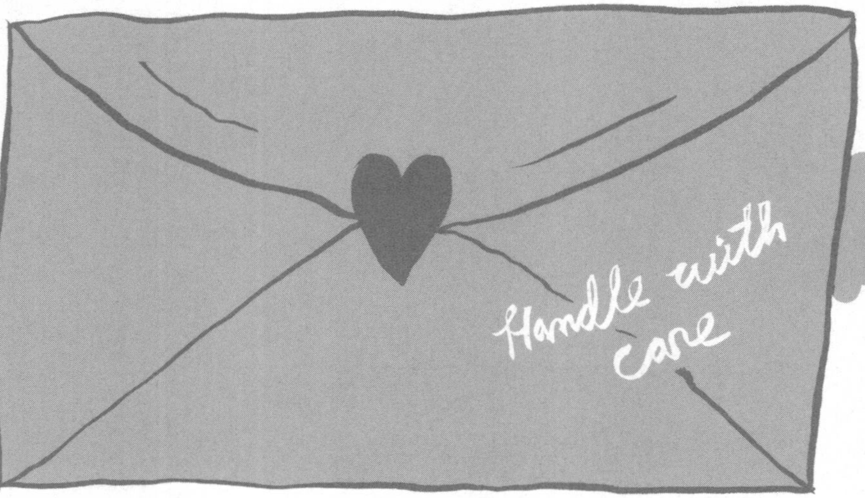

1. To write a great love letter you must allow your mind to become subservient to the rapture of your heart.
2. Love is blind, so anything you say will be seen as beautiful poetry by your lover.
3. When sealing your letter into the envelope, be sure to include glitter.
4. Most importantly, you must hand-deliver your love letter. Give your love a smoldering look as you hand it over, then, with a swoosh of your cape, fly off into the sunset.

Oh my dearest love,

Forever and ever yours,

HOW TO DEVELOP INNER STRENGTH

93

① Inner strength can be found down dark alleys and supermarket aisles.

② Developing inner strength is the same as developing a rash. Keep itching!

③ Inner strength is prone to infection. Keep rubbing alcohol nearby.

④ When all else fails, inner strength can be purchased online.

MIND OVER MATTER!! DRAW AS MANY BRAINS AS YOU CAN ON THIS PAGE!

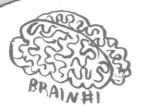

BRAIN#1

HOW TO UNDERSTAND MATH.

1 There is no need to be intimidated; math is a universal language.

✚

2 List all the human emotions you know and find their mathematical equivalent. (For example, laughter = the cosine of 55.)

÷

3 The friendlier you are to math, the friendlier it will be to you. (Keep things at "just friends." Things can get really ugly if a mathematical romance turns sour.)

═

4 Relax your brain, relax your muscles, inhale, exhale. Math can sense anxiety and tension from a mile away.

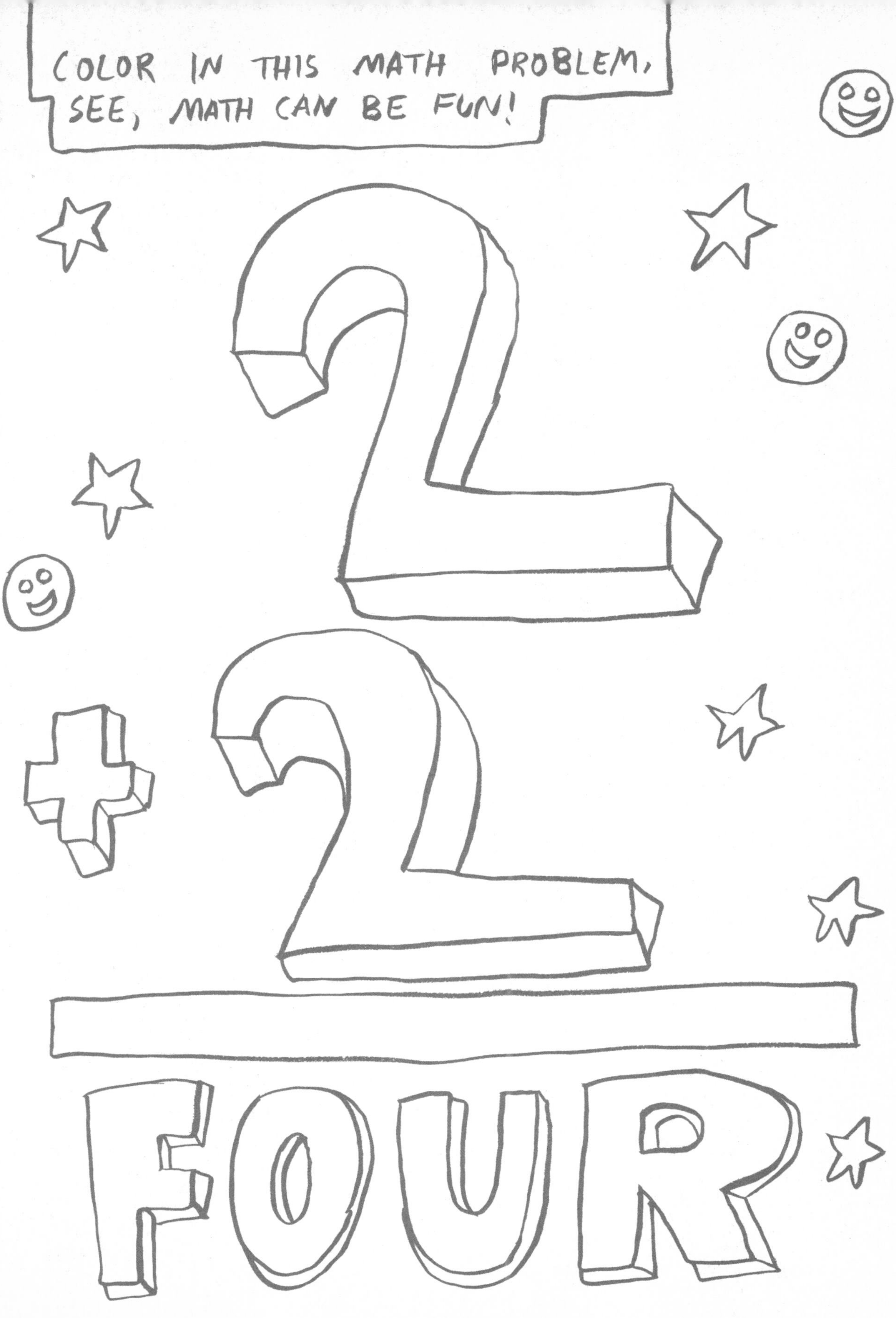
COLOR IN THIS MATH PROBLEM, SEE, MATH CAN BE FUN!
2
+ 2
FOUR

HOW TO BE REBELLIOUS WITHIN THE CONFINES OF SOCIETY.

① Join whatever counter-culture movement may be going on ... in your mind.

② Drink tap water and wear ill-fitting clothing. It's the small things.

FIGHT THE POWER (only a little)

③ Push people's metaphysical boundaries.

④ Randomly get really self-righteous, then quickly concede.

I HATE LOVE THE MAN!

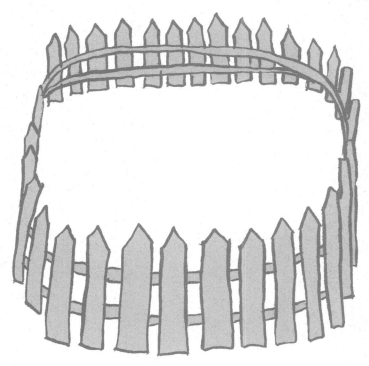

DRAW YOURSELF IN THIS FENCE.
IT REPRESENTS ALL THAT OPPRESSES
YOU IN MODERN SOCIETY.

AROUND THE FENCE, WRITE EVERYTHING
THAT IS HOLDING YOU DOWN.

ONCE DONE, DESTROY THIS PAGE.

HOW TO BECOME RICH.

1 Specialize in something obscure, then find a patron.

2 Slather your body in coconut oil, then pray to your god for money to rain down upon you.

(This has worked once before.)

3 Only befriend rich people; learn their secrets, then write a book about them.

↓

BONUS POINTS:
Become a traveling motivational speaker. This can bring in the big bucks.

4 Legally wed a million-dollar bill. Make lots of babies.

DRAW YOUR OWN CURRENCY BELOW.
PHOTOCOPY, THEN TRY TO BUY THINGS.

$100,000 coin!

HOW TO BE PATIENT.

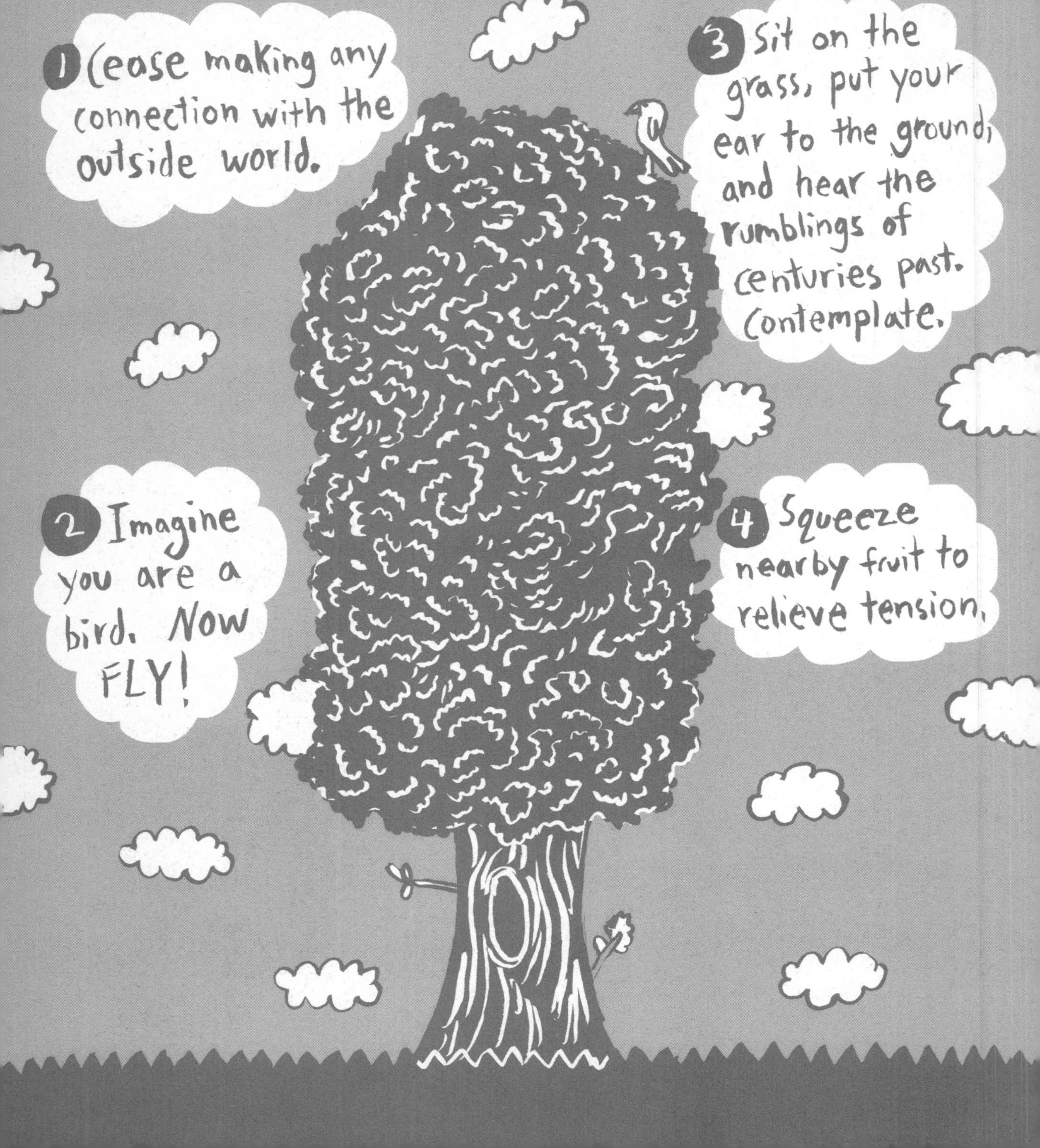

WRITE "I AM A PATIENT SENTIENT BEING." OVER AND OVER UNTIL YOU FILL THIS ENTIRE PAGE.

CONGRATULATIONS! GO TO THE FRONT OF THE LINE.

98

HOW TO BALANCE RESPONSIBILITY WITH FUN.

① Take on as few responsibilities as possible. Do not climb the career ladder and don't get near that glass ceiling. You will thank us.

② If you must be responsible, wear fun shoes.

③ Start a fun mob and a responsibility mob. Divide your time between both and make sure members never meet each other. (Dangerous results.)

④ Drink fruity smoothies during times of confusion.

FILL EACH BOWL (RESPONSIBILITY & FUN) WITH THE FUN AND RESPONSIBLE THINGS YOU DO. IF YOU NOTICE ONE HAS MORE THAN THE OTHER, DEEPLY CONSIDER YOUR LIFE CHOICES.

HOW TO BECOME THE OUTDOORSY TYPE.

① Marry someone who is, then convert.

② Leave the nature channel on while you sleep. You will be more rugged by the morning.

③ For three months, only eat food cooked on sticks over a bonfire.

↓ keep all meats rare.

↓ REALLY rare.

④ Channel your inner neanderthal. This may require you to give up shaving.

HOW TO BE A NEAT FREAK.

I will never let you go.

① This is very easy if you are growing up in a robot family.

② Get that crazy eye surgery so you have perfect vision and can spot a smudge from a mile away.

③ Start hyperventilating at the sight of a crumb. Black out at the sight of a dirty sock.

④ Be sure to give each cleaning appliance a proper burial after it passes away.

WANNA CLEAN?!

HOW TO BE MENTALLY UNBALANCED.

1 Spend too much time thinking about what you're going to eat for lunch.

Honey-roasted turkey or Genoa Ham? I just can't decide.

2 Take your brain to the brain Olympics.

3 Lie awake at night and let your mind wander. Soon enough your mind will be waiting in line at customs trying to get into Canada.

4 Chances are you will become mentally unbalanced at some point in your life without even trying. Just stay away from sharp objects.

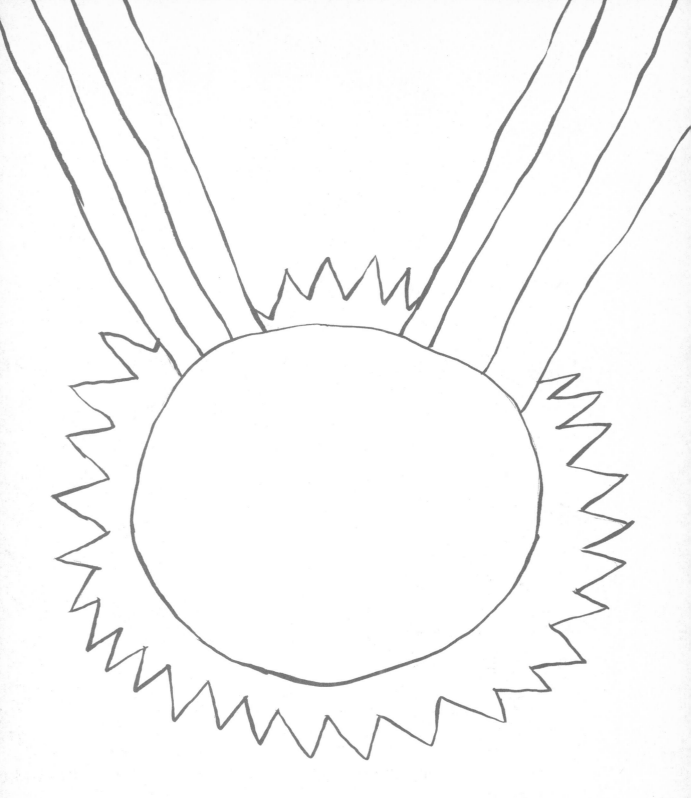

YOUR BRAIN JUST WON GOLD IN THE MENTALLY
UNBALANCED OLYMPICS! DESIGN AND COLOR THE MEDAL.

★ HOW TO FIGHT ★ THE URGE.

102

① If you feel an urge coming on, do not let it escape your body... do not let it see the light of day!

② People who live in tropical climates often have to fight off more urges. (Sorry guys.)

③ Urges can appear out of nowhere, while you're minding your own business, sitting in your chair, drinking your triple-shot espresso.

④ Doctors recommend a full eight hours of sleep and a healthy dose of self-control.

KEEP TRACK OF YOUR BATTLES!

URGE:

WIN/LOSE?:

FEELINGS:

URGE:

WIN/LOSE?:

FEELINGS:

URGE:

WIN/LOSE?:

FEELINGS:

URGE:

WIN/LOSE?:

FEELINGS:

URGE:

WIN/LOSE?:

FEELINGS:

URGE:

WIN/LOSE?:

FEELINGS:

HOW TO TALK ABOUT YOUR FEELINGS.

I HAVE SO MANY FEELINGS AND SUCH LITTLE TIME!

1 Feelings are afraid of sunlight. Talk about your feelings in dark rooms.

2 Oftentimes feelings can be contradictory. Let them battle it out in your head, but NO BLOODSHED!

3 Don't let your feelings escape too quickly. Premature feelings might have a harder time adjusting to society.

4 Allow your feelings to have play dates with other people's feelings.

The Feelings Playpen

WRITE OR DRAW YOUR FEELINGS IN THIS PLAYPEN!
LET THEM RUN WILD!

HOW TO BE MYSTERIOUS.

104

WHAT?

WHO IS THAT?

OH, SHE'S MYSTERIOUS.

AN ENIGMA!

1 Speak infrequently and dress eccentrically.

2 Try and stay in the corners of rooms. Preferably in shadowy corners.

3 Appear lost in your thoughts at all times.

4 Live in an undesirable neighborhood on the outskirts of town.

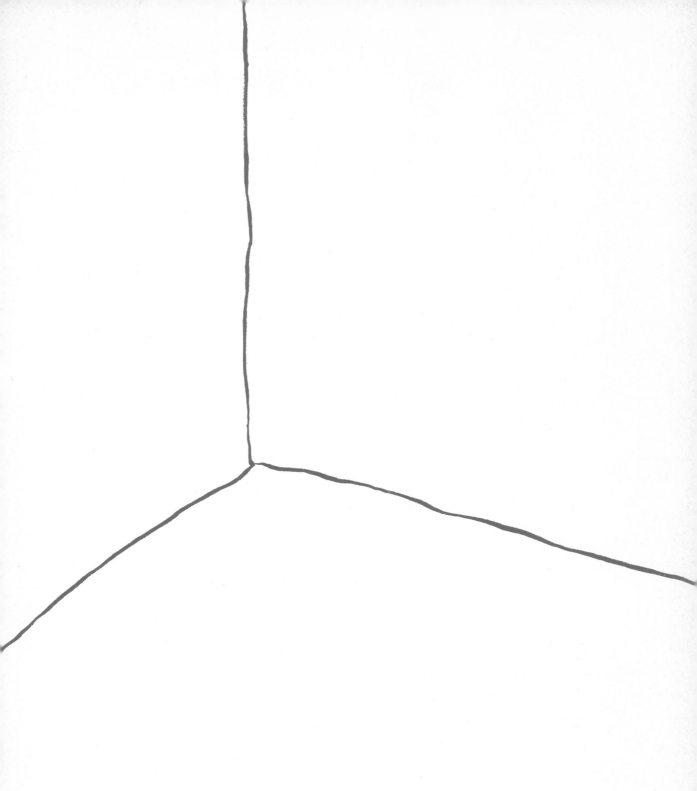

DRAW YOURSELF INTO THIS CORNER. INCLUDE THE SHADOWS.

HOW ALWAYS TO HAVE PERFECT POSTURE.

① Take a vacation to the southern tip of Malaysia; come back with perfect posture.

② Eat pine nuts, drink soy milk, convert to Judaism.

③ Take your back to group therapy sessions with other backs.

④ Get your mother to give your back guilt trips if it doesn't have perfect posture.

STRAIGHT AS A RULER !!

106

HOW TO FALL FROM GRACE.

1 Allow the wind to caress your hair ever so softly.

2 Be sure to drag every last bit of your dignity down with you.

3 Do not forget your toothbrush.

4 Wait ten years, then write your autobiography. Title it: "My Fall From Grace."

I'm ok! I'm fine... really!

IMAGINE THE DAY YOU FALL FROM GRACE. IT WILL BE
A DAY JUST LIKE ANY OTHER DAY. CREATE A MINI COMIC
ABOUT IT BELOW.

TITLE:

DATE: BY:

107

HOW ALWAYS TO HAVE THE ANSWER.

I AM A FOUNTAIN OF KNOWLEDGE.

① Remember, answers do not have to be right.

② Follow this cardinal rule: Those who are the loudest are the rightest.

③ Answers are never found in books, they are always found in your head. You were born with them.

④ Practice your "all-knowing" face in the mirror.

What is your name?

Who is the Prime Minister of Denmark?

Why do women wear lipstick?

Why do men smell worse?

When is the best time to take a shower?

How much does one whole chicken cost?

What is the purpose of higher education?

Does magic really exist?

Are babies miracles?

When should one wear a quilted vest?

Where does coffee originate from?

Why can't I feel my toes?

108

HOW TO LIVE IN THE MOMENT.

1. Ignore the fact that this may be impossible.

2. Hahahahahahahaha! Laugh!

3. Dress appropriately for the moment. You don't want to become the laughing stock of moments past.

4. Find the moment, enter it, lock the door behind you, and throw away the keys.

DOCUMENT THE MOMENT YOU ARE IN
RIGHT NOW!!! CAPTURE EVERY DETAIL.

HOW TO KNOW YOU'RE ON THE RIGHT PATH.

WRONG WAY

RIGHT WAY

1 Just keep telling yourself that any path you're on is the right one.

2 If your path is littered with false hopes and broken promises, you may be getting somewhere.

3 Whatever you do, never trust the talking dog in a suit. Any animal in human clothing is a HUGE red flag.

4 Do not be fooled by following your heart. The only true indicators of "right paths" are high-net income growth and revenue.

HOW TO WRITE AN AUTOBIOGRAPHY.

ME! ME! ME! THE STORY OF ME AND HOW I BECAME ME!! BY ME

① Keep the book's focus 100% on you. Beautiful, wonderful, intelligent, you!

② Find the overarching heroic theme of your life. If there isn't one, create it.

③ Live each day like a new chapter. If necessary, narrate your day in the third person.

④ Take creative liberties. No one will know you weren't actually the center of the universe.

☆PAGE 1: YOU'VE GOT TO START SOMEWHERE. BEGIN YOUR AUTOBIOGRAPHY BELOW.

112

HOW TO BE A LITTLE BAD (ONLY A LITTLE).

1 Allow yourself to drink diet soda.

2 On a whim, recklessly decide to buy yourself a bagel with cream cheese on your way to work.

3 Stay up late reading your emails.

4 Don't cut your fingernails for two weeks.

HEH HEH HEH

TURTLENECK

FAKE VAMPIRE TOOTH

BACKPACK FULL OF LESSER EVILS

CARGO PANTS

COMBAT BOOTS

Environmentally-safe biodegradable trash

MY TOP TEN NOT-SO-TERRIBLE SINS.

BARE YOUR SOUL! DON'T BE SHY.

113

HOW TO FALL IN LOVE.

All I can think about ...is LOVE!

long dress for long-lasting relationships

1 Have terrible balance.

2 Wear as many matching outfits as possible. Bonus points for matching tattoos.

3 Make eye contact from across the supermarket aisle, and realize you both are buying EXACTLY the same organic nectarines.

4 Run your fingers through each other's hair repeatedly. Forever.

POSTCARD FROM YOUR LOVER.

DRAW ONE BELOW.

FRONT

BACK

114

HOW TO DEAL WITH MEAN PEOPLE.

1 To prepare, wear protective armor and goggles.

2 Laughter. Mean people hate laughter.

3 Wearing pastel colors can reduce meanness in other people.

4 Build a hypoallergenic barrier of love and positivity around your person to deflect the meanies.

YOUR WORDS WILL NOT BRING ME DOWN!

WALL O' MEANIES

DRAW THE PORTRAITS OF ALL THE MEAN PEOPLE YOU COME ACROSS, THEN WRITE WHY THEY'RE MEAN.

THE DEVIL
He made me do bad things!

WELCOME TO
Adulthood
WE KNOW YOU'RE
NOT PREPARED

(115) HOW TO TRANSITION INTO ADULTHOOD.

① This transition is actually optional.

② Start lying about your age from the age of ten. If people question you, tell them you were born with a condition.

③ To practice, wear business casual every Friday, starting in middle school.

④ Reminisce about the good old days, even if the good old days involved wearing diapers.

KISS YOUR CHILDHOOD
GOODBYE. DRAW SOME OF YOUR FAVORITE THINGS FROM YOUR CHILDHOOD BELOW, THEN WISH THEM FAREWELL.

↑ VELCRO SNEAKERS
WITH LIGHTS

PICKING
YOUR NOSE

HOW TO DEAL WITH CHANGE.

1. If you're talking about the spare change in your pockets, put it in a jar. If you mean real life-altering change...you've come to the wrong book.

2. Ok, ok...we'll advise you. Your best option is to greet change with open arms. Keep the guest bedroom free.

3. Mentally prepare yourself for change by dyeing your hair a new color each week.

   "I never knew green came in so many different shades!"

4. If you really want something in your life to never change, we recommend crazy glue.

WHATEVER YOU DRAW ON THIS PAGE WILL NEVER CHANGE!
(UNLESS IT DECOMPOSES OR IS TRAGICALLY DESTROYED.)
DRAW SOMETHING HERE THAT YOU HOPE WILL NEVER CHANGE.

RELEASE THE TURMOIL!
SPILL IT ALL OUT ONTO THIS PAGE.

WHEW! DON'T YOU FEEL BETTER?

HOW TO BECOME A SHADOW OF THE PERSON YOU USED TO BE.

118

① Run, run for your life. Get as far away from you as possible.

② Write a breakup letter to yourself. It's over. Nothing will ever be the same again.

③ Only drink carbonated beverages.

④ Start a new, significantly more dull career.

THE PERSON YOU
USED TO BE.

A SHADOW OF THE
PERSON YOU USED TO BE.

DRAW!

DRAW!

HOW TO BECOME A MORNING PERSON.

1 Whether you like it or not, you will have to become a morning person. So, keep that chin up and those eyelids open.

2 Motivate yourself to wake up bright and early by purchasing those cheery morning birds who will prepare your breakfast and get you dressed.

3 Develop a crush on one of those morning news show anchors. Tune in each morning and gaze lovingly at their face.

What do you mean they don't exist?

4 If all else fails, master the art of purposeful sleepwalking.

HOW TO TELEPORT.

1 Teleporting is much easier when you're in a good mood.

2 Your particles will need a little motivation to disassemble and reassemble. Buy them a few donuts.

3 Teleportation pads are great, but your shower will work just fine. (Remember, twist the shower head to the right three times.)

4 Do not believe those teleportation diets you see on TV. No, you cannot leave fat particles behind!!

Thank you.
Thank you, everyone.

Except you.